LAYER
BY
LAYER

A PRIMER ON
BIBLICAL ARCHAEOLOGY

ELLEN WHITE

ANSELM
ACADEMIC

Dedication

It only seems appropriate to dedicate a book on archaeology
to all the precious Petrys (even though it is spelled differently) in my life.
To Sven and our children for all their love and support.

Created by the publishing team of Anselm Academic.

Cover image: © Openfinal / Shutterstock.com

Printed in the United States of America

7088

ISBN 978-1-59982-959-3

Ellen White's *Layer by Layer* is lively, info
is like sitting in on a lecture with your favo
engaged with well-chosen examples, and
keep the book grounded in the concrete r
studies, and they also help build the case
between the two disciplines. As she demo
are foundational for interpreting biblical texts. White's experience in both
disciplines makes her an ideal guide and a model of the scholarly approach
she advocates.

—Andrew Davis
Boston College

Romantic, controversial, myth-making, myth-breaking. Ellen White's introduction opens a window onto the fascinating world of biblical archaeology
and some of its most famous proponents. Every reader will have their appe-
tite whetted for more.

—Nathan MacDonald
University of Cambridge

Layer by Layer is a helpful and engaging primer on the intersection of archaeology and biblical studies. Pictures, charts, and pop culture references will
engage students while providing professors plenty of resources for the classroom. Ellen White makes a convincing case that the disciplines of archaeology and biblical studies are stronger when in dialogue. *Layer by Layer* not
only introduces the methods of archaeology, but also explores the basics of
biblical exegesis. Respect for both disciplines is evident throughout the book
and the final chapter ably demonstrates the advantages biblical archaeology
provides by considering the origins of Israel.

—Heather Macumber
Providence University

One could scarcely hope for a more helpful introduction to biblical archaeology, a field subject to much sensationalism and misunderstanding. Ellen
White explains what archaeologists really do and how their work relates to
biblical studies. Her clear writing and judicious examples will engage students
and laypeople alike. I foresee lots of students signing up for summer digs.

—Greg Carey
Lancaster Theological Seminary

Layer by Layer is an excellent companion to courses in either biblical studies or archaeology, introducing students of both disciplines to methodology
used by their colleagues that will benefit their own studies. Ellen White draws
upon her own experiences to vividly and candidly describe what it is like to
do archaeological fieldwork and what such work has contributed to answering
some of the major questions posed by the Bible. The book's lively, engaging,
and humorous style makes reading enjoyable for both students and instructors.

—Tony Burke
York University Toronto

Author Acknowledgments

There are many people to thank for bringing this labor of love to fruition. First, I am grateful to the incredible staff at Anselm Academic for accepting and supporting this project: Maura Hagarty, for seeing my vision and providing me with the resources that I needed to deliver it. Penny Koehler, for keeping the administrative elements on track. Paul Peterson, for his insights as the development editor and making me wrestle with my assumptions to ultimately produce a better book. Though no longer with Anselm full time, Brad Harmon, for listening to me talk about the need for this book for about a decade, encouraging me to pursue it, and ultimately guiding me through the acceptance process. I also thank the three peer reviewers who provided immensely helpful feedback. Finally, thanks to the Anselm production and marketing teams. It was a privilege to work with Anselm!

If gratitude could be seen and measured, then the amount that I have for Corrine Carvalho would appear as a mountain. Her guidance has made for a clearer and more useful text. Moreover, her friendship and mentorship has made me a better scholar and person! In a similar vein, I extend my thanks to John L. McLaughlin, for encouraging me to explore biblical archaeology and for his ongoing assistance and direction with my work.

Thanks also go to Hershel Shanks, Susan Laden, and the team at the Biblical Archaeology Society for exposing me to more of the biblical archaeology world and demanding nothing less than perfection. Hershel especially pushed me to do things well the first time and then make them even better, and I appreciate that. Sue gave me the freedom to take on projects and run with them, to explore and develop a vision and see it through.

When it comes to teaching and student needs, Regina Edmonds taught me more than years of courses and classroom experience. She was my much-needed rock on which I built my teaching foundation in the midst of quicksand. I am perhaps most grateful to my former students, who taught me how to teach as I tried to teach them. You all taught me about how to connect and effectively communicate often complex material. I thank you for your patience and generosity as I experimented with you.

Dan Bahat, Amihai Mazar, Nava Panitz-Cohen, and Uri Davidovich all taught me about archaeology and fueled a passion for this subject within me. Field work is not a natural fit for me, but their tutelage, dedication, and stellar teaching skills made me yearn for my trowel.

Finally, I must thank my families (birth and created) for putting up with me, supporting me, and loving me. I especially appreciate my parents, who taught me that the best way to learn something was to see it for myself (and for enabling me to do just that). And deep gratitude goes to my perfect husband, Sven, who took over parenting while I locked myself in the office for days at a time to write this book. Sven, you are a great blessing and partner; there is no one better!

Publisher Acknowledgments

Thank you to the individuals who reviewed this work in progress including:

Randall Younker, *Andrews University, Berrien Springs, MI*

CONTENTS

PREFACE

The name *biblical archaeology* may appear straightforward and, even if unfamiliar with the phrase, most people will think they understand what it means. The name likely suggests archaeology with a biblical focus and, while this was once an accurate understanding, the current model of biblical archaeology is more complex than this. Today, biblical archaeology is not a subdiscipline of archaeology but a field of inquiry that occupies the intersection between archaeology and biblical studies. Biblical archaeology is by nature an interdisciplinary dialogue between archaeology and biblical studies rather than an independent discipline. Therefore, to engage in biblical archaeology, one must become familiar with two disciplines and develop a basic understanding of the methods of both. This book provides just such an introduction.

Sometimes it is necessary to understand what something is not, in order to understand what it is. Biblical archaeology is a name that is often misunderstood and misapplied. For this reason, chapter 1 addresses common "myths" surrounding biblical archaeology and separates fact from fiction. Chapter 2 defines biblical archaeology in the modern era (post-millennium) and explores why this phrase became controversial (and remains so for some scholars).

Chapters 3 and 4 introduce the basic methods of both archaeology and biblical studies. This will help you gain insight into the primary disciplines involved in the dialogue and understand the types of data and questions each discipline produces. Chapter 5 explores the benefits of dialogue between these disciplines through an extended example that is still an open and evolving question in both fields.

This book is unique in focusing on the methods of both archaeology and biblical studies, and the method for engaging in biblical archaeology. While it uses real examples of biblical archaeology (places where the field and the text merge or collide), it is not merely a collection of such examples. This text assumes no prior knowledge of archaeology or biblical studies and explains key terms in both fields; thus it could be useful in both archaeology and biblical studies courses. This text explains what biblical archaeology is and walks the reader through how to do it, while emphasizing the foundational importance of archaeology and biblical studies.

A Note to Students

Few things are worse than being forced to read a boring book. With this in mind, I have attempted to make this one interesting as well as informative, with real-world examples, pop-culture references, and entertaining anecdotes. This doesn't mean that this text is nothing but light-hearted fun, but it does mean I have tried to make the experience pleasurable as well as meaningful. Other features designed to help facilitate learning are pictures and graphs to help you visualize some of the things described, key terms[1] (with a glossary at the end of the book) to help you identify what to study (the "these will be on the test" things), further readings to give you a starting point should your professor create assignments based on a particular chapter, and finally, study questions to help you digest the material in each chapter.

One more thing that I have tried to do is to assume nothing about you. You need not have prior knowledge of archaeology or biblical studies (including the Bible) to read this book and understand it. I have no expectations regarding your faith tradition or even whether you espouse a religious faith. Neither the interdisciplinary dialogue that is biblical archaeology nor archaeology nor biblical studies require religious faith.

A Note to Professors

I devoted ten years to thinking about this book before moving forward. Conference after conference, I would discuss with Brad Harmon of Anselm Academic what I was looking for in a biblical archaeology textbook. In the beginning, he was searching for someone to write this book and I was teaching biblical archaeology and looking for a good textbook. I remember saying, "There are good histories, there are good archaeological or biblical studies method books, and there are some detailed discovery compilations,

---

1. Each chapter's key terms are set in bold once and defined in the glossary.

but there isn't a book that does all these things." I wanted a text that introduced all of these elements and would be accessible to beginning students. I never found one, so this book is my attempt to create one.

In addition, we wanted something that would work as a supplemental text in a biblical studies course. The interdisciplinary dialogue that is biblical archaeology is often important when engaging various questions in biblical courses, but rarely are our students prepared to evaluate or even understand the relevance of archaeological finds. This text contains the basics of biblical studies methodology, an introduction to archaeological method, and a detailed explanation of how to undergo biblical archaeology, ending with an extended current example.

The pedagogical resources included to aid students will also help you design your classes, assignments, and tests. Throughout writing this book, I considered what would help me as a professor and included all the resources that occurred to me.

Independently, the disciplines of archaeology and biblical studies are enriching and rewarding. When these are brought into dialogue, one can also appreciate the contribution each makes to the other. The interdisciplinary dialogue necessary for biblical archaeology leads to better conclusions, as the hypotheses generated therein must stand up to the rigors of two demanding disciplines. By the end of this book, my hope is that it will be clear that engaging in biblical archaeology enhances one's analyses in archaeology or biblical studies.

MYTHBUSTERS

Movie legend **Indiana Jones** dashes through ancient temples battling evil foes in his quest to recover treasures from the past. Somehow he manages to defeat his enemies, win the affection of his love interest, and salvage all the ancient booty without ever picking up a trowel or setting foot in a lab. Well done indeed! This popular franchise might leave one with the impression this is what **archaeology** is all about, but actual archaeologists leave the whips and fedoras at home in their quest to learn about our ancient ancestors.

Biblical scholarship has not been embraced by Hollywood as a fascinating and sexy career. There are no blockbusters about biblical scholars defeating the latest terrorist group with their stunning ability to parse biblical Hebrew. Despite their absence from popular culture, biblical scholars know the joy of discovery and the rich reward of hard work.

These two fields—archaeology and **biblical studies**—have more in common than the media might have one believe. Both fields need each other; their relationship is symbiotic. This might not appear true on the surface. It might be easier to imagine a parasitic relationship in which biblical studies sucks the marrow of archaeology's hard-won results from the lands of the Bible. Or one might imagine the reverse is true, that archaeology can mine the Bible's historical insights, but that biblical studies transcends the truths of this world and thus has nothing to learn from archaeology.

Everyone comes to this topic with preconceived ideas, conscious or not. These opinions may be formed through the media, the language used to talk about these disciplines, a person's religious (or nonreligious) background, or other less obvious means. Some of these assumptions will be accurate and some will not. In this chapter, several of the most common misconceptions (**myths**) are exposed for what they are, even though they are prevalent and pervasive. Then biblical archaeology can be approached with a clean slate, and these disciplines and their dialogue can be explored without all the distracting external noise.

Here are six myths[1] about archaeology and biblical studies that often interfere with **interdisciplinary** research.

Myth #1: Archaeology Is Pure Science

Take a moment to picture the archaeological process in your mind (try to avoid thinking of the movie version). Likely you'll envision the meticulous fieldwork and detailed processing of a site, followed by the careful packing and transportation of finds to a sterile, technologically advanced lab for analysis. If so, good for you, as this is accurate for the most part. Yet this is only the beginning of the archaeological process. While it is true that archaeology is considered a social **science** that uses many techniques from technology and the hard sciences, archaeology is also an interpretive art.[2] The scientific initial stages provide **data**, but the data then needs to be interpreted and **interpretation** is an art. It is quite possible to misinterpret data. That's where the science of sociology enters.

---

1. The term *myth* as used here refers to something that might be widely believed but is not completely accurate. In a course on biblical studies, the term *myth* might be used in a more formal way to discuss the legends that were common in a region and the various cultural expressions of this larger metamyth. Though both uses share a similar meaning as far as accuracy goes, the first use has negative connotations because the inaccuracy is unintentional and doesn't serve a useful purpose, but the second use has positive connotations because the inaccuracies serve a useful purpose.

2. The use of technology and hard science in archaeology has grown rapidly in the last twenty to thirty years. This has resulted in subdisciplines such as metallurgy, archaeozoology, and petrographic analysis, among others, which are almost completely scientific. A good example of this scientific focus is the Scientific Archaeology Unit at the Weizmann Institute in Israel.

There are many famous historical instances of data being mis-interpreted. For example, humans used to believe the sun revolved around Earth. Modern language in reference to the sun still reflects the data that the ancients observed: "The sun rises in the East and sets in the West." The data is clear and unchanged; sometimes the sun can be observed and sometimes it can't. Therefore, the ancients determined the earth was unmoving and the sun was revolving around it. Yet Copernicus, using new instruments for measuring the movement of the planets, discovered more data that changed the long-held interpretive view. Copernicus's new data demonstrated that the previous data had been misinterpreted, not that it was false. From one's fixed position on the earth, the sun does appear to be moving, but in fact it is the earth that is moving. The first interpretation of the data was the simplest (usually the best), but the addition of incompatible data required a more complex inter-pretation. However, the introduction and incorporation of new data is where true archaeological advancement arises.

Excavations generate a plethora of data, literally millions of pieces of information that need to be processed and interpreted. Everything from the placement and number of **sherds**—small broken pieces of pottery—to the city planning of the settlement is mapped and cataloged, but this data alone says little about the civilization and those who comprised it. For example, during my first season in the field I uncovered a foundation deposit (an oil lamp nestled between two bowls under the cornerstone of a build-ing). Archaeological data shows that burying materials under the foundation of a building was common practice in ancient Israel. The data, however, does not show why people did this. Did they believe this practice would ward off demons? Did they see it as a sacrificial act to protect the building? Was it a token of thanksgiv-ing to the divine for blessing them with a new building? Was it a way to get rid of wedding gifts they thought were ugly? Was it a tradition they no longer understood themselves? Did it mean dif-ferent things at different times to different people? All of these are possible interpretations of the data. The archaeologist is looking for the best possible interpretation given the combination of available data. The process is thoughtful and serious, but not all of its aspects are scientific.

Why begin this conversation by demonstrating that archaeology is not a hard science? The reason is simple. Empty your mind of all thoughts and play the free association game. Think about the word *science* and write down every word that pops into your head. Having played this game with many groups over the years, I know that some of the most common words people say are *facts, proven, objective*, and perhaps most poignantly and dangerously *truth*. Playing the same game with the word *interpretation* leads to answers such as *subjective, opinion*, and *unreliable*. Both sets of associations are probably unfair to a certain extent, but if one begins an interdisciplinary discussion with one discipline being a *science* and the other involving *interpretation*, then one begins with a false dichotomy. This brings us to myth #2.

Myth #2: Biblical Studies Is an Act of Faith

The Bible, being a sacred text in three major world religions (Judaism, Christianity, and Islam), holds a unique position. Because of the Bible's central role in living religions, the study of its text is more complex than that of the complete works of Shakespeare or even the theological hieroglyphics of the Egyptians. With the Bible's religious role often comes the assumption that **faith** must factor into the interpretation of Scripture or that only believers would be interested in biblical studies. However, just as it is not true that only Wiccans are interested in studying the Druids or only Greeks are interested in studying ancient Greek philosophy, neither is faith a prerequisite for biblical studies. Many scholars study the Bible for reasons completely removed from faith.

What does one see when imagining a biblical scholar? A pious believer praying before meditating on a small portion of Scripture? Or perhaps a member of the clergy preparing a Sunday sermon? Maybe a dusty relic wasting away in the basement of a decrepit library as the modern world passes him by? Regardless of the image that comes to mind regarding a biblical scholar, the reality of the scholar's work is probably quite different. Biblical studies is an academic discipline subject to the academic rigor expected of all the **humanities**. Biblical studies has more in common with the study of Homer, Chaucer, and Aristotle than the message of the latest televangelist. Biblical studies is an interpretive art, but the interpretations are not based on subjective opinions. They are based on scientific data—similar to archaeology.

The data used in biblical studies differs from that in archaeology in that it is linguistic and literary rather than material; however, both disciplines begin with a set of data requiring interpretation. Here is an example from biblical studies.

The most common word in the Hebrew Bible (Old Testament) is the *waw* conjunction (the combination of a consonant [*waw* (ו)] and a vowel [*shewa* (:) or *patach* (-)]) and this word is translated in many different ways. It can mean "and," "but," "then," "or," "also," "even," and so on. Most of the time the meaning is clear from the context, but sometimes it is not and requires interpretation. One such example can be found in Song of Songs 1:5. The **genre** of this verse is an erotic love poem. The verse reads "I am black *waw-conjunction* beautiful. . . ." The data is that this word most often means "and," but those other meanings are not infrequent. The woman is talking about herself and trying to entice her lover to her. The two most common translations are "and" or "but." Yet these two meanings lead to opposite understandings. Thus the interpretation of this word in this context directly affects the understanding of this verse and the characters involved. Issues of biblical interpretation can be necessary on a grand scale or they can involve the smallest word in the Bible, as in this example. However, all interpretations begin with questions that arise from the data, just as in archaeology.

Archaeology and biblical studies are similar at their core, despite being categorized as two different types of discipline, one a social science and the other a humanities. Both disciplines generate a set of data from which questions arise, and interpretations (i.e., conclusions) are generated to answer these questions. Also, in both disciplines these interpretations require reexamination as new data arises. This new data is often generated through interdisciplinary dialogue. For example, a new discovery in archaeology can affect an interpretation in biblical studies and the reverse can also be true. Thus the data and interpretations of one discipline are important for the continued growth and development of the other.

Myth #3: Archaeology Is about Big Exciting Finds, Treasure, and Glory

One of the first questions people ask when meeting someone new is "What do you do?" When the answer is "I'm an archaeologist," this is usually met with excitement and the question, "What's the most interesting thing you have found?" An understandable question for sure but one that misses the point of modern archaeology. Archaeology today is more interested in understanding daily life in a particular place and time—the daily routine, in a way the mundane. This doesn't mean the big finds aren't valued and newsworthy; they're just not the primary purpose of investigation.

In philosophy, there is a principle that one should not make rules based on special categories (unique or unusual circumstances), but rather the rules should be based on the most common situation and special categories should be accounted for in other ways (perhaps as exceptions). The same applies to understanding ancient life. The best way to get a sense of life in the ancient world is to discover what it was like for the average citizen, to gain a sense of the majority,

© CB2 / ZOB / WENN / Newscom

The land of the Bible was known as "a land flowing with milk and honey" (e.g., Exod. 3:8), but industrial-scale honey production in the area was known only from pictographic renderings and written descriptions prior to the discovery of this tenth-century BCE plant at Tel Rehov in the Jordan Valley. Honey was used for medicine, religious ceremonies, eating, and writing.

and only after that to account for the minorities and extraordinaries. Certainly, kings and queens make interesting fodder for historical accounts, but such a small sample is not helpful in answering questions of ethnic development, evolutionary biology, or even societal structure in many cases.

Because of this, the seemingly innocent question "What's the most interesting thing you have found?" is very difficult for an archaeologist to answer. Likely, the stranger is hoping to hear something about royal jewels or an ancient palace, but the archaeologist is more likely recalling a manufacturing center, such as the honey production plant found at Tel Rehov in Israel's Jordan Valley, or a cache of administrative texts, such as those found on Elephantine on the Nile River in Egypt. For the archaeologist, the mundane *is* the dramatic.

Myth #4: Biblical Archaeology Is an Independent Discipline

The Bible includes many geographical regions (e.g., from the Middle East to Italy) and spans many centuries (at least fourteen). The sheer scope of the material and the expertise required to cover such an enormous geographic and historical span would far exceed modern disciplines, which focus on much smaller regions and time periods. In addition, the Bible is only interested in a narrow sliver of life in these places during the various time periods, and since archaeology is interested in garnering insight into the holistic lifestyle of the people being explored, the Bible would not serve as a good foundation for most ancient Near Eastern archaeological investigations. With that said, it might serve as a tool to assist in some investigations.[3]

The following chapter explores the concept of "biblical archaeology" and how that name has evolved in academic and popular understanding. For now, suffice to say, there is no one definition of biblical

---

3. Archaeological disciplines are usually defined by geographical regions (e.g., Syro-Palestinian, North American, Indo-European) and sometimes time periods, especially in areas where there is a long settlement history (e.g., Paleozoic, Classical, Islamic). This allows archaeologists to specialize in a people group and really begin to understand it (this will be explored further in chapter 2).

archaeology. For the purposes of this book, the phrase best applies to a context in which both archaeological and biblical data are involved.

Myth #5: Archaeology Is Undertaken to Prove the Bible

As the next chapter shows, in the history of archaeology there have been times when expeditions set out to do precisely this: prove the Bible, or at least use the Bible as a roadmap to understand their results. Yet most archaeologists today (or biblical scholars for that matter) have a different intent. This comes partly from a better understanding of **historiography** (as opposed to **history**) and the modern focus on daily life (as discussed in myth #3).

In the modern Western world, most people have an enlightenment view of history. When one reads history, one expects to read about things that are factually true, that is, things that actually happened in the way they are described. This statement may seem painfully obvious, but such an expectation is relatively new when one considers the entire span of human existence. In fact, even in the modern world, this expectation is beginning to be challenged as people question whether an objective account of events can be written (indeed, phrases like "history is written by the victors" note there may be more to the past than what the dominant culture recounts). In the ancient world, prioritizing fact over function was foreign. Thus, while the term *history* today typically refers to a modern practice of recording accounts of events as objectively and truthfully as possible, the term *historiography* describes the older practice of writing history to make a certain point. For example, classical historians such as Herodotus and Livy wrote the latter kind of history. Their texts are not objective, and they record events and speeches that were far removed from their experience. Historiography is free to adjust the "facts" when they do not correspond to a particular theme or purpose desired by the author.

The Bible contains many genres—law, poetry, legend, to name a few—but the overarching genre that governs them all is **theology**. Theology—literally, "the study of god(s)"—is governed by its own rules. Foremost among these is that the writing is intended to reveal something of the divine. All other genres, including those the

Christian churches consider the Historical Books of the Bible, are subject to this overarching genre.[4]

What does this mean for archaeology? Simply put, sometimes the texts and the archaeological data will be compatible and sometimes they won't. Sometimes the biblical authors are using historical facts and realities to convey their thoughts and other times they are taking liberties with these "truths" in order to present what they view as a different kind of truth.

Myth #6: Archaeology Disproves the Bible

In light of what has been discussed so far, it should be clear that archaeology does not have an agenda when it comes to the Bible (granted, individual archaeologists might, but the field as a whole does not). When what is recorded in the Bible and what archaeology reveals do not correspond, the biblical scholar is invited to explore further. For example, the historiographical book of Joshua (chapter 6) gives an account of how Israelite warriors, with seven priests and the Ark of the Covenant, under the direction of their leader Joshua and following the command of God, march around the walls of Jericho once a day for six days. On the seventh day, they march around the walls seven times, all the people shout to the sound of seven trumpets, and the walls fall down, guaranteeing the Israelites a victory. Archaeological findings from the excavations of Jericho, however, yield no wall remains from Joshua's time. Now some have argued that archaeologists should not expect to find any such remains, as the narrative is meant to indicate total destruction. Yet this "solution" will not suffice as the prevailing interpretation of the archaeology of the site is that the city was mostly unoccupied at the time of Joshua's conquest. This appears to be a case of archaeology "proving" the Bible false.

Before adopting this conclusion, however, two things must be noted. The first is that disproving the Bible was not the intention of the excavations at Jericho; if anything, the opposite was true. It is

---

4. The agreed upon Historical Books in the Christian churches are Joshua, Judges, 1–2 Samuel, and 1–2 Kings. Some Christian traditions might add other books to this list. Differing from Christians, the Jewish traditions assign these books to the category of Prophets.

probably fair to say that for every biblical element that archaeology cannot prove accurate, there is a biblical element that can be. The second thing to keep in mind is that the Bible, even the so-called Historical Books, is not intended to reveal an accurate recounting of past events but rather to provide insight into God. When archaeology appears to contradict the biblical account, the biblical scholar is presented with a wonderful interpretive opportunity. For now it is clear that the biblical author is not merely describing a situation or recounting facts, but rather taking liberties with the past in order to say something about God. When archaeology and the Bible concur, on the other hand, it is much more difficult to ascertain whether the biblical author(s) included the information for a theological purpose or a historical one.

Going Forward

Having dispelled certain common misconceptions and myths about biblical archaeology, we now turn to the methods used in biblical studies and archaeology and the ways in which these disciplines interact.

In chapter 2, the concept of biblical archaeology will be explored from its inception, through the controversies surrounding its existence, to the modern period and the variety of definitions scholars use today to define this interdisciplinary subject.

Chapter 3 will introduce the development of the basic excavation methods and the key figures in this development. It will also provide a rudimentary understanding of what happens in the field and later in the laboratories as archaeologists prepare to publish their results. Similarly, chapter 4 provides the basics for completing an exegesis—the method by which one draws meaning out of a text, which is still the backbone of most biblical scholarship and the method most used and relevant for interdisciplinary work with archaeology.

The disciplines of archaeology and biblical studies are brought together in chapter 5. Here the reader will encounter the framework for the interdisciplinary dialogue that can occur between biblical studies and archaeology. This approach to biblical archaeology will be presented through an extended current example.

Questions for Review and Discussion

1. Have you encountered any of the misconceptions described in this chapter? How so?
2. If any of these myths were familiar to you, has your thinking about them changed after reading this chapter? Why or why not?
3. How do you currently understand or define archaeology as a discipline? How do you currently understand or define biblical studies as a discipline?
4. Describe what you think the relationship between archaeology and biblical studies should be.

Key Terms

archaeology
biblical studies
data
faith
genre
historiography
history

humanities
interdisciplinary
interpretation
myths
science (social v. natural)
sherds
theology

Further Reading

Currid, John D. *Doing Archaeology in the Land of the Bible: A Basic Guide.* Grand Rapids: Baker, 1999.

Frigge, Marielle. *Beginning Biblical Studies.* Winona, MN: Anselm Academic, 2009.

Kaltner, John. *Reading the Old Testament Anew: Biblical Perspectives on Today's Issues.* Winona, MN: Anselm Academic, 2017.

Shafer-Elliott, Cynthia. *The Five Minute Archaeologist in the Southern Levant.* Sheffield, UK: Equinox, 2016.

THE BIBLE AND THE SPADE

Defining Biblical Archaeology

From its origins, **biblical** archaeology was dominated by scholars who dug "with the **Bible** in one hand and the spade in the other."[1] That is, those conducting excavations explored and interpreted what they discovered in light of what they read in the biblical text. In theory, the phrase *biblical archaeology* meant that the Bible and the **spade (trowel)** were the primary tools used by archaeologists and that both were used with equal weight. In practice, it often meant that the tools of mainstream archaeology were subservient to biblical interests.

G. Ernest Wright, one of the founders of modern Syro-Palestinian archaeology, defined biblical archaeology this way:

> To me, at least, biblical archaeology is a special "armchair" variety of general archaeology, which studies the discoveries of the excavators and gleans from them every fact that throws a direct, indirect, or even diffused light upon the Bible. It must be intelligently concerned with stratigraphy

---

1. Where this commonly used phrase originated is uncertain, but it seems to have first been uttered by legendary Israeli archaeologist Yigael Yadin (for more on Yadin's career, see chapter 3); however, it has now become a common trope that serves as a warning to archaeologists about the dangers inherent in this approach.

and typology,[2] upon which the method of modern archaeology rests; but its chief concern is not with strata or pots or methodology. Its central and absorbing interest is the understanding and exposition of the Scriptures.

For Wright the primary concern of biblical archaeology is always the biblical text. Excavations yield significant amounts of data that do not relate to the Bible and thus are of little interest to the biblical archaeologist. This understanding was considered acceptable at the time, but as archaeological methods advanced and as the discipline of archaeology became more self-reflective, the narrowness of the biblical archaeological approach was questioned and criticized.

Biblical archaeology also suffered from expansiveness. If, as Wright says, the goal of biblical archaeology is to provide insight that connects to the Bible in a "direct, indirect, or even diffused" way, then the number of sites relevant to the discipline is overwhelming. One might assume biblical archaeology would be limited to modern Israel, but the Bible refers to many places outside of this region.

The father of modern biblical archaeology and perhaps its most influential practitioner, **William Foxwell Albright**, once claimed,

> Biblical archaeology is a much wider term than Palestinian archaeology, though Palestine itself is of course central, and is rightly regarded as peculiarly the land of the Bible. But biblical archaeology covers all the lands mentioned in the Bible and is thus co-extensive with the cradle of civilization. This region extends from the Western Mediterranean to India, and from southern Russia to Ethiopia and the Indian Ocean. Excavations in every part of this extensive area throw some light, directly or indirectly, on the Bible.[3]

---

2. *Stratigraphy* refers to the settlement layers that represent the various time periods on a site, and *typology* is the idea that pieces of material culture, such as pottery, change and develop with each generation and, therefore, a type characterizes an era. G. Ernest Wright, "The Present State of Biblical Archaeology," in *The Study of the Bible Today and Tomorrow* (Chicago: University of Chicago Press: 1947), 74. To learn more about Wright and the other luminaries mentioned in this chapter, see chapter 3.

3. William F. Albright, *New Horizons in Biblical Research* (London: Oxford University Press, 1966), 1.

© dikobrazy / Shutterstock.com

Biblical archaeology, in William Foxwell Albright's broad definition, encompassed the vast area shown here. He reasoned that any discovery within the "cradle of civilization" could shed light, directly or indirectly, upon the Bible.

In Albright's day, the academic discipline known as *Orientalism* focused on this entire region and its history. To the modern academic, it may seem absurd to think that any one person could be an expert in the history, language, and culture of all the various civilizations that have comprised this extensive region.

This is precisely the objection that former American Schools of Oriental Research (ASOR) president, Eric Meyers, has to Albright's definition, which Meyers criticizes as way too broad, both geographically and chronologically. While Meyers argues it is not possible to become a biblical archaeologist under this definition, he concedes the regions and time periods are all "relevant in part" to biblical archaeology.

Duke University professor Carol Meyers points out that these other civilizations are also an important comparison point for the study of ancient Israel. She astutely observes that "because the Bible is so important in Western culture and in Christian countries all over the world, I think we can get an overblown view of what [ancient] Israel was like—compared to the megalopolises of Egypt or Mesopotamia—Palestine is really small potatoes."[4] Her point demonstrates another

---

4. Hershel Shanks, "Biblical Archaeology: Whither and Whence," *Biblical Archaeology Review* 41, no. 2 (2015): 36. This article is an interview between the editor of *Biblical Archaeology Review* (*BAR*), Hershel Shanks, and Carol and Eric Meyers. *BAR* is the widest-circulating magazine dedicated to biblical archaeology. Most of its articles

issue with the concept of biblical archaeology. While the Bible has played a vital role in shaping Western histories and cultures, the land from which it derived was not a major player in the ancient world. In many ways, it was insignificant and was often conquered and ruled by the mega-powers of the day. Therefore, one could criticize biblical archaeology for inherently emphasizing a particular land beyond its historical status and giving the impression that Israel was a dominant culture or for privileging Israelite **artifacts**. Holding Israelite archaeology next to that of the other regional ancient nations is an important perspective corrector, and necessary to prevent overinflating the significance of Israelite settlements and finds.

Carol Meyers offers a different definition for biblical archaeology: "I would say that biblical archaeology is any archaeological work that helps us understand the Bible and its **context**."[5] This definition appears even broader than Albright's, but takes on a different tone with the last six words "understand the Bible and its context." Albright omits biblical understanding from his definition; for him it is about the world that produced the Bible. Meyers, on the other hand, adds an element of textual interpretation that is closer to the theoretical understanding of the Bible and the spade. Certainly, learning about the biblical world helps one to better interpret biblical narratives.

Take Joseph's famous coat, for example. Genesis 37:3 says that Joseph's father loved him more than his brothers (he had eleven), and he showed this favoritism by giving Joseph a special coat. Many are familiar with this coat through Andrew Lloyd Webber's musical *Joseph and the Amazing Technicolor Dream Coat*. This depiction of the coat derives first from the erroneous translation in the King James Version of the Bible, which states Joseph's father gave him a coat of many colors, and second from the reality that modern sensibilities find it easier to understand why the gift of a beautiful coat would cause envy among his siblings.

Easier than what? Than understanding why a coat with long sleeves would be the object of desire and homicidal jealousy. While a

---

are written by scholars for a nonspecialist audience, and often it is the only source of interviews with famous archaeologists. These interviews and its journalistic nature make *BAR* a valuable resource for defining biblical archaeology and understanding how the current definition arose.

5. Shanks, "Biblical Archaeology," 36.

fancy-colored coat might demonstrate the wealth of the giver, a coat with long sleeves reveals the status of the recipient (at least in the eyes of the giver). Coats with sleeves are commonplace in the modern Western world, but archaeology demonstrates they would have been rare in the ancient Near East (ANE). Studying the archaeological remains of the ANE reveals that the majority of citizens primarily engaged in outdoor manual labor.

Picture an extremely hot summer day and imagine wearing a long-sleeved coat while gardening. What would you do? Probably you would immediately roll up your sleeves or remove the coat altogether. A gift of a coat with long sleeves would have been a clear statement that the giver believed the receiver didn't have to work with his hands, and for this reason, sleeves were associated with royalty in the ANE. In the case of Joseph, because the giver was his father, who held ultimate authority and power within the household, the gift was not merely a coat, but the permission to live off the work of his brothers without having to contribute to that activity himself; in other words, he was given a position of privilege.

Texts and iconography from the ancient Near East also show that this preference for a secondary son (i.e., not the firstborn son) goes against ancient tradition. The tradition of giving priority to the first-born son, known as the primogeniture, was almost sacrosanct in the ancient world. Armed with this knowledge of the ancient world, one would read about Joseph's coat in the way the author intended and understand the full significance of the gift. While a modern person might dismiss a gift of a long-sleeved coat, an ancient person might respond with awe. As expansive as Carol Meyers's definition is, she defines biblical archaeology as an interdisciplinary dialogue rather than a lens through which one discipline views the other. Meyers's understanding is the basis for the modern concept of biblical archaeology.

The phrase *biblical archaeology* has developed in its meaning. Rarely now is it used to refer to the archaeological **subdiscipline** that focuses on ancient Israel and the surrounding nations. This subdiscipline is usually referred to as Syro-Palestinian archaeology or the archaeology of the Southern Levant.[6] This follows the convention

---

6. The use of these terms to refer to the subdiscipline is not universal. There are still a few universities and scholars who continue to refer to the subdiscipline as biblical archaeology, but this is becoming increasingly rare.

across the field of archaeology of naming subdisciplines according to chronology or geography. Biblical archaeology in the modern context refers to an interdisciplinary dialogue between biblical studies and archaeology. This is sometimes confusing as the original use did refer to an archaeological subdiscipline, but as has been demonstrated that understanding of the phrase was both too broad and too narrow to be accurate. Biblical archaeology's transition, from being the name of an archaeological subdiscipline to referring to an interdisciplinary dialogue, was gradual and controversial.

The Bible Becomes Controversial

The growing concern that *biblical archaeology* (as a name for a sub-discipline in the field of archaeology) was a way of imposing the Bible on archaeology led some archaeologists to want to abandon the term altogether. Particularly vocal in his disapproval of the continued use of the phrase was **William G. Dever**, the former director of the **W. F. Albright Institute for Archaeological Research** in Jerusalem. His position was that the phrase *biblical archaeology* implies "that there is a particular brand of archaeology whose function is to confirm the Bible."[7] Dever claimed the historicity presented in the biblical text was irrelevant for archaeological analysis, and also that archaeological investigations of history were not useful for biblical studies. He viewed textual historiography as an independent lens on the past, and biblical studies as a matter of faith rather than academic investigation.[8] Dever explained further,

Beginning more than 30 years ago, my own agenda—for better or worse, always right "upfront"—has been simply to "secularize" our branch of archaeology. In other words, (1) to eliminate the longstanding biases resulting from theological, political, and cultural presuppositions; (2) to create an

7. William G. Dever, "'Biblical Archaeology' or 'The Archaeology of Syria-Palestine,'" *Christian News from Israel* 22 (1972): 21.

8. William G. Dever, *Recent Archaeological Discoveries and Biblical Research* (Seattle: University of Washington Press, 1990). More recently, Dever's position might have changed and he may be more accepting of the phrase *biblical archaeology*, but with qualifications and not as an independent discipline.

autonomous, professional discipline that could take a respectable place within the mainstream of Near Eastern archaeology; and above all (3) to foster a dialogue between this newly independent branch of archaeology and biblical studies, not a monologue as previously, in the belief that each discipline needed and could benefit from the other.[9]

Dever's final point is important to note. Even those who have expressed concerns regarding the name *biblical archaeology* view the dialogue between biblical studies and archaeology as beneficial. Dever did not object to the idea that the two fields had something to say to each other, he objected to the relationship (and sometimes practice) implied by the use of this name.

The controversy surrounding the name arose in the 1970s, and by the 2000s it seemed the dissenters had won the day. This led Ronald Hendel, the Norma and Sam Dabby Professor of Hebrew Bible and Jewish Studies at the University of California, Berkeley, to claim,

> If one looks around today, it seems that biblical archaeology has been mostly abandoned. The historical and intellectual structure that William Foxwell Albright and others constructed has been shaken and lies mostly in ruins. Archaeology did not illumine the times and events of Abraham, Moses, and Joshua. Rather, it helped to show that these times and events are largely unhistorical. The more we know about the Bronze and early Iron Ages, the more the biblical portrayals of events in this era appear to be a blend of folklore and cultural memory, in which the details of historical events have either disappeared or been radically reshaped. The stories are deeply meaningful, but only occasionally historical. Archaeological research has—against the intention of most of its practitioners—secured the non-historicity of much of the Bible before the era of the kings. . . . Biblical studies and archaeology have had a divorce.[10]

---

9. William G. Dever, "Whatchamacallit," *Biblical Archaeology Review* 29, no. 4 (2003): 57.

10. Ronald S. Hendel, "Biblical Views: Is There a Biblical Archaeology?," *Biblical Archaeology Review* 32, no. 4 (2006): 24–36.

At the turn of the millennium, it seemed that Hendel was correct and biblical archaeology was dead. For example, when preparing the Oxford encyclopedia on this subject, the publishers wanted to call it *The Oxford Encyclopedia of Biblical Archaeology*, but the editors found they were having trouble getting submissions from those working in predominantly Muslim countries. Because of this, the name was changed to the *Oxford Encyclopedia of Archaeology in the Near East*—the name the published version bears—and the problem of contributions was solved.

In 1998, the **American Schools of Oriental Research (ASOR)** changed the name of its magazine from *Biblical Archaeologist* to *Near Eastern Archaeology*. This change was made despite 80 percent of the membership voting against it. **Eric Meyers** explained the effects of this change in the organization, saying, "It kind of left biblical archaeology in a corner, at least in ASOR. While biblical archaeology still has its place, it's a limited place." These changes in the linguistic mindset were the result of decades of discussion and at times outright feuding.

By the 1970s, there was growing discomfort with the phrase *biblical archaeology* to describe the archaeological endeavors undertaken in countries that formed the ancient Near East (mostly in the region today referred to as the Middle East). Some of the criticism was about who was engaging in the research, especially as more professional academics (rather than clergy) became involved, but the issue was more than professional bias.[11] Using a phrase containing the

---

11. Ordination or clerical vocation is not an impediment to preforming good archaeological investigation; there are many terrific archaeologists who also have church/faith credentials. The objection was to those who had no training in archaeological method or were engaging in excavation as a faith exercise rather than a vigorous study. There is a particular concern when it comes to financing an excavation. Often there is a sense of obligation to a donor, and since many faith-based institutions have historically been interested in funding biblically related excavations, there were concerns this might affect archaeologists' interpretations of their findings. The famous archaeologist Leonard Woolley, the original director of the Ur excavations, understood the connection between the Bible and money and shamelessly exploited that knowledge: "He particularly emphasized the connection between Ur and Abraham in works aimed at the public; in his scholarly contributions, he was much more circumspect, focusing instead on Ur's cultural history, social structure, architecture, art, and technology. Unlike some of his counterparts working in the Near East, Woolley did not set out to prove the historicity of the Old Testament, but he fully exploited any possible links between the Bible and archaeology. This is not surprising given his flair for

word *biblical* implies the discoveries found at these sites are limited to a biblical connection, and this is not true of the expansive histories of most sites. There are several ways in which this criticism was fair. If the discipline is called *biblical archaeology*, then it will naturally attract people who are interested in the Bible in ways that the name *Syro-Palestinian archaeology* would not. In addition, as with so many things, money was also a factor. It is no secret that digs with a biblical connection tend to receive more donations than those without. This sounds like a positive thing and perhaps even a good argument for retaining the name *biblical archaeology*, especially in tight economic times. However, rarely does money come without strings attached, and many of these donors may have certain expectations regarding what their money will find at the site. This could consciously or subconsciously affect the way in which the archaeologists interpret what they find.

Moreover, the name *biblical archaeology* is just inaccurate. Take, for example, the site of the ancient city Tel Rehov. This city is not mentioned in the Bible and no biblical event unfolded there; however, it was occupied during many of the biblical periods, which would place it within the parameters of biblical archaeology. The discoveries made at this site can certainly shed light on life in ancient Israel and may even shed light upon various common practices that are mentioned in the Bible, but to define the site and all its finds by this tenuous biblical connection seems unjust. The same could be said for sites that are mentioned in the Bible—Beit She'an, a neighboring city to Rehov, for example. According to 1 Samuel 31:10, the body of King Saul was hung from the walls of Beit She'an, and in 1 Kings 4:12 the city is listed as part of the territory of Solomon. However, this is the extent of the biblical references to this large ancient city, whose history spanned from the Egyptian occupation to the Roman period and beyond. Can the extensive and important history of this city truly be limited to its meager biblical connections? The short answer is no.

---

publicity and perpetual need to raise funds to continue excavations at the site—funds far more readily available for projects with biblical connections." Edward M. Luby, "Backward Glance: The Ur-Archaeologist," *Biblical Archaeology Review* 23, no. 2 (1997): 24–36. With the rise of university funding and secular scholarly sources, the pressure of faith-based money was somewhat alleviated in the 1990s, but money is never abundant and more recent cutbacks across the board are causing a resurgence of this concern. See, e.g., Candida Moss and Joel Baden, *Bible Nation: The United States of Hobby Lobby* (Princeton: Princeton University Press, 2017).

© ChameleonsEye / Shutterstock.com

Old-school biblical archaeologists tended to focus on the biblical strata of a site and ignore the non-biblical strata. Often, however, much of a site's importance lies outside the biblical period. Beit She'an, for example, receives two brief mentions in the Old Testament but was a thriving metropolis in the Roman period, as its Roman remains, shown here, attest.

Ebla

The excavation of the site of the ancient kingdom of **Ebla** brought such discussions to the forefront. Located in the predominantly Muslim country of Syria—a country with many important biblically connected sites, such as Damascus and Aleppo—Ebla turned into the perfect storm for biblical archaeology. According to the great Israeli archaeologist Yigael Yadin, shortly after the Ebla controversy, biblical archaeology became "taboo," a "dirty word" in Syria.[12] What happened at Ebla certainly contributed to this general feeling. At least one scholar writing for *Biblical Archaeology Review* wrote about Ebla using a pseudonym, because he was afraid of professional retaliation when trying to work in Syria.[13]

Between 1974–1976, one of the most extensive literary finds from the ancient world was uncovered in Ebla. It began with just

12. Hershel Shanks, "*BAR* Interviews Yigael Yadin," *Biblical Archaeology Review* 9, no. 1 (1983): 16–23.

13. Adam Mikaya, "The Politics of Ebla," *Biblical Archaeology Review* 4, no. 3 (1978): 2–6. (The citation here is to the author's published pseudonym as that is what appears in the publication.)

forty-two tablets (usually enough to excite and invigorate any excavation) in 1974, but in 1975 more than 16,000 additional tablets were discovered, and in 1976 a further 1,500 tablets were found. Ancient writings are an extremely rare find and are always deemed significant, but an archive of this magnitude is headline news. Ebla was originally settled circa 3500 BCE, but "the age of the archives" extends from circa 2400 to 2300 BCE. Most of the tablets are royal administrative texts, others are lexical (word lists most likely used for instruction), mathematical, or magical inscriptions. Some of the tablets were reported to contain biblical connections.

One of the roughly 17,500 tablets found at Ebla is shown here. Early excitement regarding the relationship of these texts to ancient Israel led to controversy and questions regarding biblical archaeology as an independent discipline.

These biblical connections sparked the imagination of the Western media and were further fueled by eminent scholars, such as David Noel Freedman, who claimed the discovery was "more significant for elucidating the Hebrew Bible than any other archaeological discovery ever unearthed."[14] This is quite a stunning statement from someone who had worked directly with the Dead Sea Scrolls. The publicity attracted the attention of the two leading professional societies, ASOR and the **Society of Biblical Literature (SBL)**, in various ways. For a time, it seemed a major breakthrough had been made for archaeology and biblical studies, an **intersection** properly understood as biblical archaeology.

The connections included a creation and a flood narrative; references to cities also mentioned in the Bible (Salem, Hazor, Lachish, Megiddo, Gezer, Dor, Sinai, Joppa, and Jerusalem); an Eblaite king named Ebrium or Edrum, which might be a **cognate** (a related

---

14. Mikaya, "The Politics of Ebla," 2.

or connected word) of Eber (a distant grandson of Noah), or even more tenuously connected to the word *Hebrew*; the language was said to be proto-Canaanite and thus in the same linguistic family tree as Hebrew; references made to gods named El and Ya (which could relate to the short form of Yahweh, the personal name of God in the Old Testament); biblical personal names are found in the texts (Abram, Esau, Israel, Michael, Saul, Ishmael, and David); kings are anointed; and prophets appear.

Keep in mind these tablets considerably predate the Bible so none of these connections could have derived from those Scriptures. Early on in the analytic process, dig director Paolo Matthiae was quoted in the *New York Times*, saying, "We have found the civilization that was the background of the people of the Old Testament. . . . The Ebla tablets establish the patriarchs and their names as historical realities. . . . They seem to show that many Hebrew ideas and words came from Ebla."[15] The *London Observer*'s Chaim Bermant reported that "[Giovanni] Pettinato [the epigrapher—writing expert—for Ebla] believes that King Ebrum may have introduced the worship of Yahweh some two or three centuries before Abraham. He also suggests . . . that the Israelites were derived from Syria. . . . All of which may show that Jews may be aboriginal Syrians." As time progressed, both Matthiae and Pettinato denied all biblical connections to Ebla and referred to such theoretical connections as "pseudoscientific mystifications." Some believed this change of heart was due to pressure from the Syrian government to disavow all biblical connections or else face difficulties with further excavations in Syria.

No intimidation or threats by the Syrian government have been reported, however, and there seems to be no evidence of official intimidation. In fact, one member of the translation and publication team, University of California Los Angeles Professor Giorgio Buccellati, said, "I can assure you the Syrians are not concerned with any biblical connections that the Ebla materials might reveal. Places like Ugarit and Mari are in Syria and have been extremely important in biblical studies, but the Syrians have never expressed concern over this. Any scholar suggesting a political element in the interpretation of Ebla materials is tilting at

---

15. Alvin Shuster, "Discovery of an Ancient City in Syria Called 'Sensational,'" *New York Times*, October 25, 1976.

Significant Archaeological Sites in Syria

© Peter Hermes Furian / Shutterstock.com

windmills."[16] While the texts found at the sites Buccellati mentioned are often used for understanding the ancient world and the Hebrew Bible in particular, the difference with Ebla is that scholars began to talk about Syria as the birthplace of the people who became Jews as a historical reality and not a literary backdrop. This is a radical difference, with sociopolitical implications that extend beyond cross-cultural comparisons.

Dr. Sabah Kabbani, the Syrian ambassador to the United States during this controversy, stated, "The matter is of concern because of the statements of Mr. [Menachem] Begin [then prime minister of Israel] and his Likud Party. Mr. Begin is trying to use the Holy Bible as a real estate register. Today he wants the West Bank. In a few years it may be Aleppo or Damascus."[17] Harvey Weiss, the director of the Yale University Archaeological Project in Syria, echoed this sentiment:

---

16. Mikaya, "The Politics of Ebla," 3. Ugarit and Mari are both sites where large written archives were discovered. These texts have been influential in biblical studies for the insight they provide into the world behind the Bible.

17. "Syrian Ambassador to US Asks *BAR* to Print Ebla Letter Rejected by *New York Times*," *Biblical Archaeology Review* 5, no. 5 (1979): 15–17.

Avowedly publicity seeking statements by "biblical archaeologists" in this country, however, have obscured the nature
of this discovery and have focused public interest on the
belief of "biblical archaeologists" that the cuneiform texts
of Ebla verify the historicity of the biblical patriarchs and
point to Ebla as the "home" of the Hebrews. Given the
abuse of other ancient texts by Israeli politicians to justify
their retention of Syrian and Palestinian territory, it should
come as no surprise that Syrian officials wish to protect the
Ebla texts from a similar fate.[18]

This statement by Weiss demonstrates the hostility that was developing toward the phrase *biblical archaeology*. Here he hurls the name
biblical archaeologists as if it were a negative slur that should invoke
shame. Weiss, himself an archaeologist of the region, is clearly dis-
associating from the phrase based on what he views as the illegiti-
mate practices of those who use it. Stripping away the hysteria and
important historical politics of this particular situation, the concern
raised is that the fragment (a handful of tablets among thousands)
becomes the focus, rather than a puzzle piece to the whole. The situation at Ebla served as a real-world example of the theoretical issues
raised by the dissenters that was played out on an international stage
due to the major media interest.

What Is Biblical Archaeology Today?

The past challenges in defining *biblical archaeology* still exist, but a
more open discussion of the concerns and definitional limitations
seems to have made the phrase at least palatable to most, and some
parameters have been agreed to. Yet a universally accepted definition
remains elusive.

Some, like Hershel Shanks, the editor of *Biblical Archaeology
Review*, responded to charges that old-school biblical archaeology is
irredeemable, saying, "We should recognize our failures. We should
recognize the limitations of our evidence. But we need not concede
that in our search we are doomed at the outset to biased results. Nor

---

18. Ibid.

must we abandon the enterprise altogether."[19] All disciplines grow and evolve their methods, but rarely does this result in a new discipline or a name change. These changes demonstrate progress, not death.

These changes are not limited to specialization but also include the methods and questions used in these specialties. The esteemed Harvard professor Frank Moore Cross confessed that at Gezer, an archaeological site located midway between Jerusalem and Tel Aviv, they used to throw away bones rather than study them. When the discipline began, it was about finding cities and confirming major events.[20] Today, it is about daily life and long-term environmental changes—what Carol Meyers calls "household archaeology." These

Andrew Shiva / Wikimedia / Israel-2013-Aerial 21-Masada.jpg / CC BY-SA 4.0

Masada, Harrod's palace-fortress near the Dead Sea, played a significant role in Judean history, particularly during the First Jewish Revolt. Yet, if one focused solely on its biblical connections, these historic events would be of only marginal interest.

---

19. Hershel Shanks, "Should the Term 'Biblical Archaeology' Be Abandoned?," *Biblical Archaeology Review* 7, no. 3 (1981): 54.

20. For the methodological development of biblical archaeology, see chapter 3.

changes can give the impression it really is a new discipline, but some see this evolution as proof the discipline is healthy, not dead.

Sites like Masada, an ancient palace-fortress near the Dead Sea, make defining biblical archaeology difficult. Masada is not a biblical site, as far as it is not mentioned in the Bible. Yet it served as a fortress-palace for Herod the Great, who does play a role in the Bible and ruled over land described in the Gospels. Because of this, the results of the Masada excavations could help illuminate the backdrop of the Gospels. Yet Masada also served history in another capacity as the location of the final stand of the First Jewish Revolt, which occurred after the events described in the Bible. It is clear this site must not be excavated in a way that limits the results to the illumination of the biblical text at the expense of its other contributions, including to the history of Judaism, revolutionary response theory, and Roman military tactics, to name but a few. A definition of biblical archaeology must account for sites such as Masada and not transform one of the disciplines into a subset serving the other.

Therefore, biblical archaeology is not a discipline but rather an interdisciplinary endeavor that takes place in the intersection between biblical studies and the various subdisciplines of archaeology.

Questions for Review and Discussion

1. What would you say is the largest potential danger in doing biblical archaeology? Explain your answer.
2. Do you think the name *biblical archaeology* should have been abandoned altogether? Why or why not?
3. What do you think is the biggest challenge for biblical archaeology today?

Key Terms

William Foxwell Albright	Bible
artifacts	biblical
American Schools of Oriental Research (ASOR)	*Biblical Archaeology Review*
	cognate

continued

Key Terms *continued*

context
William Dever
Ebla
intersection
Carol Meyers
Eric Meyers

Society of Biblical Literature
  (SBL)
spade (trowel)
subdiscipline
W. F. Albright Institute for
  Archaeological Research

Further Reading

The best reading for chapter 2 is *www.BASLibrary.org*, a subscription archive of the Biblical Archaeology Society (BAS). In its more than forty-year history, it has covered the discussion regarding the name *biblical archaeology* and the issues and controversies involved. BAS publishes *Biblical Archaeology Review* (*BAR*), the biblical archaeology magazine with the highest circulation. *BAR* is written by scholars for the general public. Readers will encounter key scholars in these ongoing discussions and references to further material on this topic.

ARCHAEOLOGY 101

Great endings don't always have auspicious beginnings. When the father of biblical archaeology, Sir **William Matthew Flinders Petrie** (1853–1942), died at the ripe old age of eighty-nine, he bequeathed a most unusual gift to the Royal College of Surgeons of England: his head! This behavior may appear eccentric, but perhaps it is appropriate for the man who transformed archaeology from sloppy treasure hunting to a meticulous, scientific field (though not single-handedly).

Petrie excavated more than fifty sites and wrote ninety-eight books, but began life not alive at all. Stillborn on June 3, 1853, he was saved by a fast-acting and experienced nurse. He pulled through only to be dropped on his head by another nurse. As a child, he was afflicted with chronic asthma so severe he could not attend school. His mother, Anne Flinders Petrie, was a gifted linguist who had taught herself Hebrew, Greek, Latin, German, French, and Italian, but Petrie did not inherit her talents. He later confessed he had made no less than ten attempts to learn Latin and five or six to learn Greek. This history might signal to some that Petrie was not suited for academic life, but others can see his tenacity coming through. Ultimately, it was this perseverance that made his **excavation** methods rise above the rest.

While his best-known find is probably the Merneptah Stele, Petrie's lasting contributions to the field are theoretical rather than methodological.[1] Two contributions are of particular note: a shift

---

1. For more on the Merneptah Stele, see chapter 5.

in focus from major archaeological finds to what Petrie called the "unconsidered trifles," particularly pottery, which has become the bread-and-butter of ancient Near Eastern digs, and recognizing the importance of stratigraphy, the sequence of habitation layers that are found in an excavation.[2]

Petrie connected these two major contributions to archaeology, while excavating at the Southwestern Israeli site of Tell el-Hesi in 1890. At Tell el-Hesi, the stream of the Wadi Hesi had eroded one entire side of the *tel* (a large hill-like mound that forms as habitation levels, or strata, accumulate), exposing the site's stratigraphy. Petrie surveyed this side of the excavation and collected enough pottery from each stratum to demonstrate that the form of pottery evolves from one level of stratum to the next. This phenomenon is called typology. From this discovery, he developed a system he called "sequence dating," sometimes called the pottery clock. While his particular method is no longer in use, the principle and theory behind it is; in fact, pottery is a major resource for dating strata prior to the use of coins. Also unusual, Petrie published the results of his work immediately. The problem of publication remains a major issue

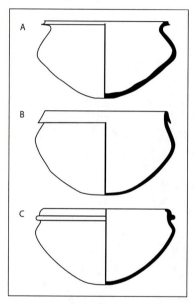

Changes in pottery styles over time are known as *seriation*; such changes are useful in dating strata (i.e., **sequence dating**). Illustrated here are cooking pots dating to (A) the Late Bronze Age through Iron Age I, (B) early twelfth century to the mid-eleventh century, and (C) mid-eleventh and tenth centuries.[3]

---

2. Petrie was not the first to "discover" stratigraphy, as it had been previously noted in 1870 by Heinrich Schliemann, the German archaeologist who excavated at Troy.

3. Sketches adapted from Adam Zertal, "Israel Enters Canaan—Following the Pottery Trail," *Biblical Archaeology Review* 17, no. 5 (1991).

Archaeological Periods

Archaeological Period	Interval
Neolithic	9000–4500 BCE
Chalcolithic	4500–3500 BCE
Early Bronze	3500–2000 BCE
Middle Bronze	2000–1550 BCE
Late Bronze	1500–1200 BCE
Iron I	1200–1000 BCE
Iron II	1000–586 BCE
Iron III	586–539 BCE
Persian	539–322 BCE
Hellenistic	322–63 BCE
Roman	63 BCE–325 CE
Byzantine	325–636 CE

in biblical archaeology, largely due to the massive amounts of data generated each season (i.e., the period of time spent excavating each year) and the way in which excavations are funded.

What would become archaeology began in earnest as a hobby quest in the early nineteenth century by adventurers, engineers, and biblical scholars to uncover places mentioned in the Bible. In 1838 and 1852, Edward Robinson (1794–1863) of Union Theological Seminary in New York, initially in conjunction with American Protestant missionary Eli Smith (1801–1857), managed to correctly identify one hundred biblical sites using only a compass, a thermometer, a telescope, measuring tapes, a thorough knowledge of Arabic, and the Bible. These two scholars, however, did not understand the nature of tels and, therefore, overlooked many sites. The British Royal Engineers, under the leadership of notables such as Charles Wilson (1836–1905), Claude Conder (1848–1910), and

Levantine Archaeological Sites Discussed in Text

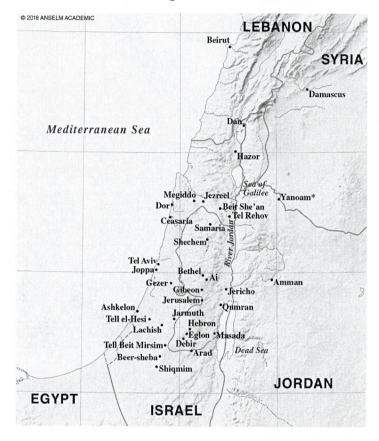

© 2018 ANSELM ACADEMIC

LEBANON

Beirut

SYRIA

Damascus

Mediterranean Sea

Dan

Hazor

Sea of Galilee

Yanoam*

Megiddo   Jezreel

Dor   Beit She'an

Ceasaria   Tel Rehov

Samaria

Shechem

River Jordan

Tel Aviv

Joppa   Bethel   Ai

Gezer   Amman

Gibeon   Jericho

Jerusalem   Qumran

Ashkelon   Jarmuth

Tell el-Hesi   Hebron

Lachish

Tell Beit Mirsim   Eglon   Masada

Debir

Beer-sheba   Arad   Dead Sea

Shiqmim

JORDAN

EGYPT

ISRAEL

Horatio H. Kitchener (1850–1916), during the 1870s conducted surveys of the entire Palestinian area. These archaeological investigations, which examined the surface area of a region to gain information about a site's history, resulted in the twenty-six-volume work *Memoirs*, which includes photographs, plans, and a large map. Conder and Kitchener's seven-volume survey remained the basis of all topographic maps until the establishment of the state of Israel in 1948.

Ground surveys were not the only type completed at this time. Near the Temple Mount, British engineer Charles Warren (1840–1927) became an accidental archaeologist when stationed in Jerusalem by the **British Royal Engineers** in 1864. Much of his commissioned work occurred below ground. This reflects the nature of development in an ancient civilization—one generation builds on top of the previous generation, thus creating a civilization mound, or **tel**. Warren discovered many features of ancient Israel, including an arch that once led to the entrance of the Second Temple, which was destroyed by the Romans in 70 CE. As a result of such finds, the **Palestinian Exploration Fund** was established by Queen Victoria in 1865, and two years later Warren returned to Jerusalem for further, official excavations. To map the **topography** of ancient Jerusalem, Warren tunneled more than a hundred feet underground and created twenty-seven narrow shafts. Unfortunately, during Warren's time there was no way to reliably date the artifacts he uncovered.

A major contribution to the refinement of method came from George A. Reisner (1867–1942), Clarence S. Fisher (1876–1941), and David G. Lyon (1852–1935) and their excavation at Samaria from 1908–1910. Reisner is credited as the first to carefully separate the various strata and make a meticulous effort to preserve the details of each find. He did this with photography, maps, and architectural plans, writing descriptions of each piece on an official finds registry, and keeping a daily diary. Many of these techniques are still in use today. Often referred to as the **Reisner-Fisher Method**, horizontal or architectural excavation dominated the field until the introduction of the vertical method fifty years later.

William Foxwell Albright (1891–1971) is often referred to as the "father" or "founder" of biblical archaeology. This son of missionaries excavated as if the Bible was true history; this is also what he taught his students, many of whom went on to become famous scholars in their own right.[4] For the most part, Albright excavated according to the horizontal method—digging large areas of one level of stratum across the tel—but at Tell Beit Mirsim, he also experimented with the vertical method, which allows one to investigate multiple strata in a smaller area. While doing this vertical experiment, he devised subdivisions of the standard three **ages** (Stone Age, Bronze Age, Iron Age) that were specific to the Levant (a large region bordering the

---

4. His famous students include George Ernest Wright, Frank Moore Cross, and David Noel Freedman, all of whom have legacies that continue to influence biblical studies and archaeology.

eastern Mediterranean); these subdivisions are still used with some refinement today.

One of Albright's students, G. Ernest Wright (1909–1974), staffed his excavation of Shechem (a city named in the Bible) with graduate students, a practice that in subsequent generations morphed into *field schools*—places where students come to learn methodology in a hands-on environment. Prior to this, large-scale excavations were performed by an almost exclusively paid, local labor force with little or no archaeological training. From this first introduction, these field schools enlisted a predominantly **volunteer** staff (those who pay a fee to excavate; students often receive course credit for an additional fee); this practice has become the norm.[5]

Arguably the most famous female biblical archaeologist is Dame **Kathleen Kenyon** (1906–1978). Best known for her excavations in Jericho and Jerusalem, Kenyon began her career in Britain working with Mortimer Wheeler. It was on Wheeler's excavations that the method of digging five-meter by five-meter **squares** with one-meter **baulks** (the earth that archaeologists preserve between squares) was devised. Kenyon brought this method with her when she joined the Joint Expedition of Samaria (1952). This vertical—rather than horizontal—method was revolutionary. Known as the **Wheeler-Kenyon** method, it transformed field excavation and remains (with some variations) the dominant method used in excavations.[6]

Yigael Yadin (1917–1984), born into archaeology as the son of renowned archaeologist Eleazar Sukenik (who purchased the Dead Sea Scrolls on behalf of the State of Israel and first connected the community there with the Essenes), understood the power of the media and politics for the success of archaeology. Some might argue that the dissemination of archaeological results is beyond the scope of methodology, but this is shortsighted. How one presents findings is often as important as the findings themselves. Perhaps in tacit recognition

---

5. The excavations at Gezer under the direction of William G. Dever are often credited with the development of field schools, and it is true that those excavations made the notion popular, but the practice originated at Shechem.

6. Mortimer Wheeler (1890–1976) specialized in Iron Age and Roman archaeology in Britain. Kenyon worked with Wheeler at Verulamium (north of London) and at the London Institute of Archaeology, which Wheeler founded. Wheeler first developed the method and Kenyon exported it to the land of the Bible.

Excavated squares surrounded by undisturbed earth (baulks) show that the Wheeler-Kenyon (or "vertical") method is being employed in this excavation.

of this, often finds of interest to a popular or general audience appear in print long before the technical and academic reports are published.[7]

Due to his background serving as chief of staff to the Israel Defense Forces and deputy prime minister to Menachem Begin, Yadin was in a unique position to understand the impact of media and politics and to use both to his advantage. He has been touted as the Israeli Albright due to his approach and often began excavations with a text in mind (though not always the Bible, as his use of Josephus at Masada demonstrates).[8] Determined to find a claim for the Jewish occupation of Israel by using archaeology to "prove" the narratives in Jewish literature as historically true, Yadin advertised everything he uncovered with a connection to the Bible.[9]

---

7. Kenyon, for example, produced two books about Jericho that targeted the general public but did not manage to publish a formal report before her death. Another reason for delays in formal scientific reports is the massive amount of effort needed to produce such a report on an excavation. Such reports often appear decades after the excavations they describe.

8. The first-century Roman Jewish historian Flavius Josephus wrote a famous account of the final stand of the Jewish soldiers at the end of the First Jewish Revolt. According to Josephus, these soldiers barricaded themselves in the fortress-palace atop Masada and ultimately committed mass suicide rather than fall to the Romans.

9. The effects of Yadin's talent for this type of interpretation and dissemination can perhaps be viewed as part of the backdrop for the Ebla crisis discussed in chapter 2.

Under the direction of William G. Dever (1933–) and Joe Seger (1935–), the American Excavation at Gezer (1964–1974), a joint expedition of Hebrew Union College and the Harvard Semitics Museum, introduced onsite **specialists** and the use of a core staff to field work. These additions led to more meticulous and specialized records but also contributed to the sheer mass of material that needs to be prepared for **publication**, a task further complicated by the number of people involved in its initial recording.[10]

Modern Methods

The Principles

What makes one location desirable for habitation at one period in history likely makes it a good place to settle at another time, especially if the original reason is due to natural resources, such as water and fertile soil. Because of these factors, it is common for places to be inhabited generation after generation. When occupation takes place over centuries, the build-up of time can be seen in layers, called strata, which ultimately result in a mound, or a tel, which can look like a hill to a casual observer. One can still observe this process occurring today.

Picture yourself driving through an older residential neighborhood. You notice a small house stripped to its foundation, to allow rebuilding with a different footprint. Elsewhere, you see a few large, new houses interspersed with smaller, older dwellings. This sort of construction and reconstruction has literally been happening for centuries. One generation wants to live where another has, but the material culture of the previous owners, in this case a house, does not meet the needs or taste of the younger generation, so they rebuild to suit their desires. In the language of archaeology, where new inhabitants used the foundation of a previous house, the foundation is the older stratum and the new building is the younger. Layers closer to

---

10. This short history of methodological developments is limited to the region associated with biblical archaeology (though that is a complex idea, see chapter 2). For a brief, broader sketch of the archaeologists who formed the holistic discipline, see Brian Fagan, ed., *The Great Archaeologists* (London: Thames & Hudson, 2014).

Stratigraphy is the study of successive habitation layers at an archaeological site. Multiple strata are evident in this image from Area D of Tel Rehov in the Jordan Valley. Across the middle of the image are a series of foundation stones, which are dug into the remains of an older mud brick wall (the lines of the bricks are still visible).

the surface are always younger layers, as they developed after the deeper layers. This understanding is important when dating strata. Imagine two hundred years from now an archaeologist excavating this house. During that investigation she finds a brick in the foundation with the date 1950 stamped on it. From this find, she knows that everything found in the levels above this brick must be younger than 1950, but if she digs through that foundation and finds the remains of a wall, that wall will be older than 1950.[11]

Several things can complicate the interpretation of strata. The ancients dug pits into even older strata for a variety of reasons, such as the disposal of garbage. This causes a problem, because those older

---

11. This applies to the stratum rather than the individual finds within the stratum. Just as in modern times, people in the past kept heirlooms and keepsakes that could be passed down through generations. These finds, however, would be rare for two reasons. The first is that heirlooms by nature are few in number as they are a specially selected item, meant to be unique and hard to come by. The second is that people rarely leave behind their treasures. Next to living beings, the first things usually packed or saved are one's cherished items. Therefore, it would be unusual indeed to find them discarded in an excavation unless the stratum resulted from destruction or disaster.

layers are now missing the dug portion (likely distributed elsewhere on the tel in a younger stratum), and because younger material is often inserted into the older strata. A similar issue occurs with fills that occur naturally or, more often, were human-made to level ground for construction. These are an issue, because the material used to fill is often taken from another part of the site and could contain elements of other strata, such as wash caused by water or erosion that moves remains from one part of the tel to another. Burials and rebuilding can also remove strata from one place and put it in another.

Strata should not be confused with **occupation levels**. When one buys a house today, it is not always with the intention of knocking it down to build something else. Often, when a family buys a home they redecorate a bit and then move in. Think, for example, about the trend to convert old industrial factories into condos and lofts. No new buildings are erected and many of the original **features** are maintained, but other structures or features are added and a new purpose is given to the old building. The factory now has a new occupation level. When a structure is built with longevity in mind, then it is often more logical to reuse and repurpose what already exists than to start afresh. In biblical archaeology, Masada is a particularly good example of this. Originally a lavish palace used by King Herod the Great, who had a reputation for opulence, Masada was later used as a fortress by Jewish soldiers attempting to withstand a siege by the Roman army.

When archaeology first developed the horizontal method of excavating (also known as a clearing excavation or the Reisner-Fisher method), the work dominated the landscape. The horizontal method is simple and logical; one excavates large areas, particularly those associated with architecture or even the entire site, to a selected level of stratum. This approach to early practices of biblical archaeology is sensible, given the primary purpose of most of its practitioners: to discover more about the biblical period and perhaps confirm biblical narratives as history. In an effort not to miss anything "significant" in the desired stratum, one must dig the entire level. Advantages of this type of excavation are that it accurately provides the extent of the site and recovers the architecture.

One site where the horizontal method was used is Gezer (mentioned in Joshua 21), which was dug under the direction of R. A.

Ellen White

King Herod the Great was famous for his opulence and for his palace-fortress Masada; he spared no expense. This can be seen in the detailed colored frescos and elaborate floor tiling (against the far wall) that extend below the later added stone structure. This wealthy display represents the first occupation layer. The stone structure is an industrial size oven, which was added by the Jewish rebels during the First Jewish Revolt. The rebel remains are the second occupation level.

Stewart Macalister (1870–1950) from 1902–1905 and 1907–1909.[12] Unlike his contemporary Reisner, Macalister was not meticulous and was the only archaeologist on site with a crew of four hundred workers, which meant that he could not possibly oversee every aspect of the excavation work. Macalister also showed little concern for **stratigraphy**. Subsequent excavations have demonstrated significant flaws in his conclusions.

One example of these flawed findings involves Macalister's conclusions regarding a find at Gezer. While digging at Hazor, Yigael Yadin had uncovered a city gate, and later when excavating

---

12. Macalister did excavate in trenches but with the goal of exposing the Hellenistic city of Gezer (though his inattention to stratigraphy caused him to misdate many features), and his focus was on the architecture with little regard to what surrounds it. For a detailed description, see Samuel R. Wolff, Gary Arbino, and Steven Ortiz, "Macalister at Gezer: A Perspective from the Field," *http://www.telgezer.com/gezer/assets/File/Mac%20Gezer%20article.pdf.*

at Megiddo, had discovered a similar gate, both of which he dated to the Solomonic period (tenth century BCE). Yadin was familiar with 1 Kings 9:15, which claims Solomon built similar structures in Jerusalem, Hazor, Megiddo, and Gezer. Having found two of the four gates, Yadin was interested to know whether a similar gate could also be found at Gezer. Yadin turned to Macalister's writings and found reference to a Maccabean fortress (second century BCE) that he thought sounded like it could actually be the remains of a city gate. Yadin contacted the new excavation directors at Gezer, who sure enough found the remains of the second half of a city gate and Yadin's theory was confirmed. In this case, it was lucky the records were good enough that Yadin was able to see past Macalister's faulty Maccabean fortress interpretation to develop a new theory, and the new expedition could revisit the area. However, this subsequent reevaluation leads one to speculate about those times later archaeologists have not been so lucky; it also shows the value of being able to revisit a site at a latter period when more data is available.

Often in a horizontal excavation only a very limited area is explored vertically to provide insight into the stratigraphy of the site. This does not give an accurate picture of the history of a site in general, however. The major disadvantage of the horizontal method is that it becomes impossible to reevaluate the results of previous excavations using modern methods and technology. Prior archaeologists used the best methods and technologies available, but as science advances so too do methods and results. Since archaeology is destructive by nature—one must remove what is found to proceed to the next older level of stratum—it is essential to preserve some area for the future. This preservation is perhaps the most important feature of the vertical method and one reason it has become dominant in the field.[13]

The vertical method (also known as the Wheeler-Kenyon method) examines a site by squares and excavating the full stratigraphy of a site. This method leaves an area around each square, known as

---

13. There are exceptional sites for which for a variety of reasons the horizontal method is still the better choice, such as Caesarea, because it developed horizontally rather than vertically. In other words, instead of later generations building on top of the previous, as at sites like Caesarea, the city developed beside what was there in the past (similar to the modern concept of urban sprawl).

Excavation Methods at Megiddo

Megiddo is a site of biblical and archaeological importance. The book of Revelation identifies Armageddon (Greek for *Har Mediddo*, "Mount Megiddo") as the site where kings will gather before the final battle. Megiddo, which has been excavated for over one hundred years, provides examples of both horizontal (see top image) and vertical (see bottom image) excavation. In the top image, of

Horizontal excavation at Megiddo

© Courtesy of the Oriental Institute of the University of Chicago

Vertical excavation at Megiddo

© Courtesy of The Megiddo Expedition

continued

Excavation Methods at Megiddo *continued*

the so-called "Solomon's Stables" excavated by the University of Chicago's Oriental Institute (1925–1934), the entire stratum has been exposed; all material above this layer has been removed. As a result, the removed layers are no longer available for study, which is unfortunate as this level at Megiddo has become very important for understanding the chronology of the region, and according to leading Israeli archaeologist Israel Finkelstein dates to the time of King Omri, not Solomon. The bottom image depicts the modern excavation of Area Q, which uses squares and baulks (unexcavated earth) preserved between each. This will allow future archaeologists to revisit the site and reexamine the interpretations of the current team.

---

a *baulk*, which, crucially, provides an opportunity for future archaeologists to explore the same site using more evolved methods and technologies.

The ability to revisit a site is a major advantage. There are other advantages to the vertical method as well. First, as previously discussed, the strata that relate to the Bible have historically generated the most interest; however, the biblical region has a rich and extensive history after the biblical periods as well. Because the vertical method tends to open smaller areas and is committed to documenting, recording, and to some extent preserving each stratum, the younger layers are better preserved. Historically, the Bronze and Iron Ages have been the most explored strata in Israel, but perhaps in a hundred years archaeologists will have a greater interest in the Islamic period, which is chronologically later than the biblical period and thus would have been mostly destroyed by the horizontal method (often by scholars who were not specialists in this era). Second, on a practical level the vertical method requires fewer staff and less equipment to excavate than the horizontal method. If one is opening a smaller area, fewer resources are required to complete the task. Because modern archaeologists are interested in daily life and the common (some might say average) experience, rather than the extraordinary, they do not need to worry about not uncovering every find or architectural feature because they didn't excavate the entire site. Today the quest is for the social anthropology of the site rather than its treasure trove (though those are still exciting to find!).

The Practicals

The Parts

Since the majority of digs now use the vertical method of excavation, one of the first decisions that must be made is where to start. Excavators may choose to open multiple areas if they have a larger site, but if it is a small dig they may choose to start with one area. Note that *area* is the technical term for a section of a site under excavation. Areas on digs are often assigned alphabetic letters as their name (e.g., Area A, Area B, etc.). Each area has its own dedicated field team. The size of the area varies even on a single excavation.

Several factors are considered when choosing which areas to dig, such as topography (the layout or arrangement of the physical features of a region), insight into the stratigraphy of the site, and results of site **surveys** or ground-penetrating radar. Tel Rehov in the Jordan Valley provides a good example of the first two factors. With both an upper and lower mound, this topography made it logical to open areas on each elevation. The different topological levels at Tel Rehov also made it necessary to open an area on the side of each mound to explore the stratigraphy in detail. Area D was opened on the sloping side of the lower mound, while Area B was located on the upper mound. Both were required to be excavated as the settlement patterns (reflected in the stratigraphy) might differ for each part of the

Topography is a factor at Tel Rehov in the Jordan Valley, where the city was built upon two naturally occurring elevations. The two mounds had to be treated differently as the stratigraphy developed uniquely on each. Area D, which is under the large black tarp on the left of the image, identified the stratigraphy of the lower mound. A separate area (B), which is not depicted, identified stratigraphy for the upper mound.

tel; it was especially necessary to determine if these separate elevations occurred naturally or artificially.

Surveys and **imaging technology** are the most common means of determining where an area should be opened. Previously, archaeologists had to rely on ground surveys to determine the best places to open areas; however, modern imaging techniques are removing some of the educated guesswork. For example, the site of Shiqmim in the Wadi Beersheva is extensive (more than twenty-four acres) and contains ten hills; it is one of the largest Chalcolithic (4300–3300 BCE) sites in the Negev desert region in southern Israel. During the 1989 excavation, a subterranean village located underneath the site was uncovered.[14] This naturally led to questions about the size and scope of the village. The site was far too large to excavate in its entirety (not to mention how destructive that would be), so the directors, Tom Levy and David Alon, decided to use geophysical diffraction tomography (GDT), which uses sound waves to generate computer images of underground features, to explore one of the hilltops considered to be representative of the others. The result was a 3D image of a "honeycomb of subterranean Chalcolithic architecture." Physical excavation later demonstrated the accuracy of the image.

In a vertical excavation, within each area, excavators open squares. A square is what it sounds like, a perfectly square piece of ground, usually five meters by five meters, although the size may vary. The excavators will cordon off this area, usually with sandbags, and dig into the stratigraphy, but not outside the marked area. Areas often contain several side-by-side squares with preserved ground—baulks—in between the squares. The baulks are not excavated, but left in place to give a visual representation of the area's stratigraphy and to preserve part of the area for future archaeologists to revisit.

When one starts excavating a square, usually the entire square is given one **locus** number.[15] Locus numbers were invented by Israeli

---

14. The site of Shiqmim historically had above-ground and below-ground settlements. The reason for the underground complexes is still debated and options range from defence to storage to burial chambers. It is also debated whether the above- and below-ground structures were in use simultaneously or whether they represent the initial phase of the settlement.

15. When walls or features can be seen on the surface prior to excavation commencing, these would be assigned their own locus numbers from the start.

army officer P. L. O. Guy while working at Megiddo, in order to provide the precise location of finds.[16] *Locus* means "place" or "spot" in Latin, and it is an appropriate term because locus numbers are used to direct scholars to the exact location on the excavation that a given find was found. Then when a change occurs, usually from uncovering a feature—an archaeological element that is a part of the site, such as a wall—a new locus number is assigned after measuring the exact dimensions. For example, when a wall is discovered, a new locus number is created for the wall and the earth on each side of the wall. When an artifact is discovered, it is recorded with its area, square, and locus number. Ideally, from the recorded data on each find, a reader of the excavation report could theoretically map the site.

Architectural elements that cannot be easily removed from a site, such as walls and built-in ovens (*taboons*), are usually assigned a number of their own and recorded separately from finds and loci. Some archaeologists refer to all such architectural elements as **installations**, while others use the term *installation* to refer to only some architectural elements, such as walls.

Anything that is uncovered and can be removed from the site is considered a **find**. Some finds are extremely common, such as pottery sherds (broken pieces of pottery). Others, such as inscriptions or precious metals, are quite rare, which is why they are called special finds. **Destruction strata** are particularly valuable from an archaeological perspective, because of the number of special finds they yield. Unlike an abandonment stratum, in which the inhabitants most likely left by choice with enough time to pack things that were precious to them or that they used the most, destruction layers often preserve things as they were (*in situ*), and thus provide the archaeologist with more information about life in that place. Pottery sherds, though common, are valuable to archaeologists because they help with dating the strata. Coins offer even better dating information, but were not yet in general use in the earlier periods that biblical archaeologists study. For periods that pre-date the use of coins, pottery provides the most common dating clues.[17]

---

16. Guy was also the first to take aerial photographs of a site by attaching a camera to a balloon. He later became the Chief Inspector of Antiquities for the Mandatory Government.

17. There are some exceptions to this, such as when one has enough organic material to perform an expensive carbon dating test, but the vast majority of strata

The Tools

Certain archaeological **tools** are universally used on land excavations, and that is unlikely to change in the near future. The main tools are trowels, pickaxes (large and small), brooms and dustpans, and buckets. The vast majority of work at an excavation involves "going down" a few inches at a time. Initially, one starts with a pickax and then moves to trowels and brooms to level the area, using buckets for everything from dirt removal to find storage. Most volunteers will never need to use any additional tools.

There are, however, many additional tools that are used at various points. Some of these are mundane, such as shovels and wheelbarrows, and others are iconic, such as sifters (which come in wet and dry forms and are particularly helpful for small finds, such as jewelry and seals). While not commonly associated with archaeology, large construction equipment is also used on some dig sites. These tools are useful in two major ways: (1) to quickly establish the stratigraphy, especially if a site developed on a naturally occurring hill; (2) to remove large architectural elements, especially in a city that contains stone structures. At the opposite end of the size scale, dental tools are sometimes used, particularly to excavate the insides of vessels that were found complete (i.e., still intact, as opposed to sherds that can be restored).

Technology is always increasing the number of useful archaeological tools.[18] One area in which this is particularly true is that of imaging. The Jezreel Expedition used LiDAR—a form of radar that uses laser light—to map three square miles around the site of Jezreel in order to identify areas for further survey and potential excavation. As archaeologists are now sensitive to being as nondestructive as possible, the use of ground-penetrating radar, magnetometry, and resistivity allow large areas of a site to be explored from the surface,

---

in this period are still dated by the pottery found. Willard Libby, a Nobel Prize winner, invented radiocarbon dating, known as Carbon 14 or C14, in 1949. It has become a valuable resource for archaeologists, as it can provide a scientific range for dating various strata. Within biblical archaeology, this technology has led to the high and low chronology debate between key players Amihai Mazar of Hebrew University and Israel Finkelstein of Tel Aviv University, respectively. For more information about high and low chronology, see, Israel Finkelstein and Amihai Mazar, *The Quest for the Historical Israel* (Atlanta: Society of Biblical Literature, 2007).

18. A complete list of technological tools is beyond the scope of this discussion and, due to the rapid pace of technological advancement, would quickly become outdated.

which then allows the dig director to target where to dig or whether to excavate at all. These noninvasive technologies will likely continue to expand and archaeological method will adapt to their use.

Reflection Transformation Imaging (RTI)—sometimes in connection with Multispectral Imaging (MSI)—is one of the photographic advancements being used to better analyze artifacts. This technology takes many images of an artifact under many different light angles and combines them to allow the user to manipulate the image for the best possible reading. Multispectral imaging adds various wavelengths to the light used (e.g., infrared and ultraviolet).

Bruce Zuckerman, as the director of the West Semitic Research Project and InscriptiFact Digital Image Database Library, which contains more than 1.5 million images, continues to push the boundaries of photographic possibilities. One example of where this technology has been helpful is in relation to the debated ivory pomegranate. In

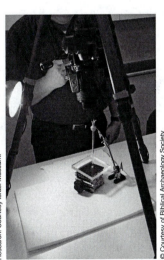

This tiny ivory pomegranate was celebrated because the divine name (Yahweh) appears to be inscribed upon it. It was later declared a forgery by the Israel Antiquities Authority and removed from display at the Israel Museum, but renowned Sorbonne epigrapher André Lemaire still champions its authenticity. Due to its small stature, it is difficult to see the miniscule details even with a microscope, but the use of Reflection Transformation Imaging, pioneered by Bruce Zuckerman of the University of Southern California, has allowed experts to see the disputed area clearly and the debate to continue.

1981, the esteemed Sorbonne epigrapher André Lemaire wrote an article in the *Revue Biblique* that introduced a small (about an inch and a half tall) ivory pomegranate that appeared to have the divine name Yahweh written on it. The pomegranate had a suspicious history and was an unprovenanced find, coming from the antiquities market rather than being found *in situ* on a professional excavation. More recently, a study by the Israel Antiquities Authority (IAA) claimed the inscription is a forgery, and the Israel Museum has removed it from display. One of the primary issues for the epigraphers is whether one of the letters (*a taw*) extends into a break (if not, it would be evidence of forgery), but this is unclear with the naked eye even aided by the use of microscopes. The RTI images do reveal the extension into the break, however, and thus the debate continues.

Thomas E. Levy and his Integrative Graduate Education and Research Traineeship for Training, Research, Education in Engineering for Cultural Heritage Diagnostics (IGERT-TEECH) developed "cyber-archaeology," which seamlessly and digitally combines archaeology, computer science, engineering, and natural sciences. In Levy's model, everything from radiocarbon dating to Geographic Information System (GIS) to portable 3D scanners to cloud technology are fully integrated into his (and University of California San Diego Professor Mohammad Najjar's) completely digitized excavation of the Edom Lowlands Regional Archaeological Project, a site in southern Jordan. Levy states the major contribution of this technological method is speed in all four domains of the archaeological process: data acquisition, curation, analyses, and dissemination. What used to be a manual collection and correlation of data is now a digital process, with computer technology putting the pieces together. This cyber-collusion provides rapid communication for all the technological tools used on the site and rapid data access for those who interpret and analyze the data. For example, their pioneering use of a Total Station (or Electronic Distance Measurer EDM) and GIS to collect X, Y, Z measurements (latitude, longitude, and elevation) at a site not only gave each feature a unique geospatial number but also readied the excavation for 3D visualization and virtual reality technology.

Like most things, the internet is changing how archaeology is done. One example of this is the emergence of cooperative **databases**. These databases allow a scholar in one place to upload into a database

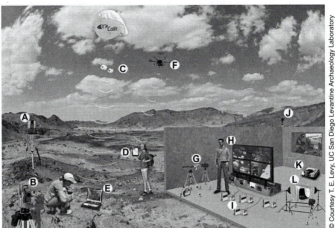

This mock-up of technologies used by the University of California San Diego and Department of Antiquities Jordan excavation team demonstrates the emerging reliance that archaeologists have on technologies and the benefits they bring to field work: (A) LiDAR, (B) total station, (C) helium balloon photography, (D) OpenDig database for recording the work of the registrar, (E) ToughBook computer providing wireless connection to cameras, (F) Octo-Copter, (G) handheld X-ray fluorescent analyzer providing nondestructive elemental analysis, (H) OptiPortable display wall, (I) portable 3D scanners, (J) differential GPS base station, (K) Fourier transform infrared spectroscopy for mineral analysis, and (L) digital photography lab.

specific information that a user in a different part of the world can then view and immediately use (rather than waiting for large and expensive tomes to be published and housed in only the largest research libraries). The digital nature of these databases is also an advance, as the quality of images is vastly superior to a printed picture. An excellent example of this is the Levantine Ceramics Project (LCP) (*www.levantineceramics.org*), created by Andrea Berlin of Boston University to facilitate international cooperation in the study of pottery. The LCP states, "Our focus is on ceramics of all eras— from the Neolithic era (c. 5500 B.C.E.) through the Ottoman period (c. 1920 C.E.)—produced anywhere in the Levant, which includes the modern nations of Turkey, Syria, Lebanon, Cyprus, Israel, Jordan, Palestine, and Egypt. Our goal is to build a digital resource that makes it simple to submit, share, search for, refine, and use ceramic evidence." This unique project continues to use cutting-edge technologies to promote mass sharing of large amounts of data. Due to the importance of pottery in the study and understanding of the ancient world, this is an invaluable resource that is leading the way for future collaborative sharing projects.

The Staff

Every archaeological investigation has a dig **director** or, especially on larger excavations, dig codirectors. The directors are the lead academics who apply for the permits and funding and oversee the entire process in the field and lab. The directors are responsible for setting the research agenda for a site and determining the extent of the excavation (in size and scope). They are also the ones who primarily liaise with external bodies, such as sponsors, investors, and the media. Historically, the dig directors are the voices and faces of the excavation, but this is morphing due to the rise of specialized subfields, and a team approach is becoming more common. In the team approach, each specialist is responsible for certain aspects of the dig, with the dig directors serving to oversee and synthesize the overall data.

Specialists are scholars and scientists who focus on one particular element within an excavation. Some of these specialists have been present on excavations for a long time, such as photographers and epigraphers. Others, such as archaeozoologists and botanists, began to be a part of excavations after being included at Gezer when Dever was director (1964–1974). Still others have been added as subfields expand or are created; digital graphing experts and imaging specialists are good examples here. At times these specialists might participate in multiple digs to answer regional questions rather than site-specific inquiries. For example, regional studies are good for answering questions of population and migration. The development of cooperative databases is also important for this type of regional analysis; this is part of the reason the creation of such a database is an explicit goal of the Jezreel Valley Regional Project (*http://www. jezreelvalleyregionalproject.com/goals%2c-methods%2c-theory.html*).

Each area will have a **supervisor** who oversees the work taking place in the entire section. Depending on the size of an excavation, there may be other supervisors (per square or stratum) in the area under the direction of the area supervisor. Usually the area supervisor is responsible for the daily **site maps** (hand or digital drawings of what the area looked like at the end of each day), which map the location of loci and the progress of each individual square. While the supervisors oversee the entire area, they usually also personally excavate (whereas a director or specialist may or may not, or may do so only in complicated cases). The field lab usually also has a supervisor, though the title for the role differs depending on the excavation. Often a large part of this position is administrative and organizational, but usually this person also conducts the first phase of processing finds (marking pottery, cataloging basic data on special finds, etc.).

The **registrar** is also an administrative role, but this person's role is exercised in the field. Depending on the site, there might be one overall registrar or each area might have its own registrar. Registrars record everything that happens on site. Each bucket is recorded and every find is labeled. Registrars also generate locus numbers and feature numbers (e.g., a new wall is found and the registrar will record it and assign it a call number). All of this used to be done by hand but, more often than not, now the registrar(s) will enter the data directly into computers, especially since computers are now durable enough to withstand the often harsh conditions of the field.

The bulk of the labor is done by volunteers, often students, the level at which almost all senior staff start out. Volunteers usually pay for the privilege of the archaeological experience. Some are students who are looking for course credit or field experience, others are simply members of the interested public who want to know what it is actually like to dig. Diverse is the best word to describe the role of volunteer, both in terms of the activities they will undertake and who participates. Volunteers come from all over the world and represent a full spectrum of adult ages and backgrounds. They may be asked to do anything from pickaxing to taking levels to sifting.

Life on a Dig Site

What one can expect to experience on an excavation is standard.[19] A dig day starts early, probably around 4 a.m. Volunteers are expected to get up, dress properly (no sandals on a dig site), and have some

---

19. Some variations to the schedule proposed here do exist but are not significant.

breakfast before gathering and traveling to the dig site. If the workers are not camping onsite, they will usually arrive by 5 a.m., when it is just light enough to see. In the cool of the morning (*cool* being a relative term), the work gets started in earnest. For six to eight hours the actual excavation occurs, with a short break for a second breakfast. Around noon the staff will return to their dwelling place for lunch and a chance to escape the hottest hours of the day.

Between lunch and 3–4 p.m., there is often free time for the volunteers (many take a nap to rest their weary bodies and escape the heat), while the senior staff meet to discuss the results of the day's efforts. This is also a good time to update site drawings—top plans and section drawings—and records. By midafternoon, staff members are usually expected to attend **pottery washing**, in which the pottery from the previous day that has been left to soak in water is scrubbed with nail brushes to expose any distinctive features (markings, writings, coloring); sherds with inscriptions on them are known as *ostraca*. After pottery washing, the previous day's washed pottery is read, which

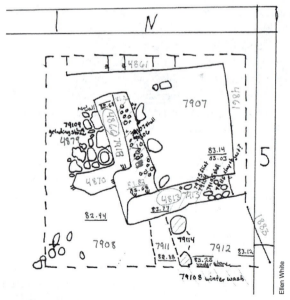

Section drawings, which may be produced by hand or using a computer, visually represent each day's progress on the dig. Each drawing includes the loci found in a square along with elevations and finds.

entails counting the number of sherds for each type of pottery—a type being the style of pottery that can be attributed to a specific date period and geographical region. Pottery is then sorted according to **diagnostic sherds** or pieces (rims, handles, bases), unusual sherds, and discard pieces. Since sherds are the most common find in this region, the vast majority of a volunteer's day is dedicated to ceramics; this highlights the importance of these seemly innocuous finds.

The day concludes with dinner, which is often followed by a lecture on some element of archaeology relating to the site; these lectures are commonly given by the dig directors or specialist staff members, but guests occasionally present.

The schedule is demanding, but usually excavation only occurs five days a week, with the other two dedicated to rest and tourism (many digs offer day trips on the weekends to other significant sites, accompanied by expert guides). Many of the large excavations host a weekly site tour that allows staff from one area to see the progress being made in other areas and get a sense of the overall expedition.

It would be a misunderstanding to believe that when an excavation season is over, the work has ended; in fact, it is really just beginning. There is so much work involved in processing finds and analyzing data after returning to the lab that excavations often alternate between seasons in the field and in the lab (e.g., one year in the field and the next year dedicated solely to working with the material already uncovered). All of this must take place before publication of any results from the excavation, which is why the process is so lengthy.

Questions for Review and Discussion

1. In learning about archaeological methods, past and present, what things surprised you?
2. Name the advantages and disadvantages of both the vertical and horizontal methods for excavation.
3. What makes the study of sherds vital for the archaeologist?
4. What are some of the advantages of modern archaeological methods? Are there any disadvantages? If so, name them and explain.
5. What changes might be on the horizon for archaeology with continued advancements in technology?

Key Terms

Ages (Stone, Bronze, Iron, etc.)
areas
British Royal Engineers
baulk
database
destruction layer/stratum
diagnostic sherds
director(s)
excavation (expedition or dig)
feature
field school
finds (common v. special)
imaging technology
installations
Kathleen Kenyon
locus (loci)
occupation levels/layers
Palestinian Exploration Fund
William Matthew Flinders
   Petrie
pottery washing and sorting

publication
registrar
Reisner-Fisher method
   (horizontal or architectural
   archaeology)
sequence dating
site map
specialists
squares
stratigraphy (strata, stratum)
supervisors
surveys
tel
tools (common, large, small,
   technical)
topography
volunteers
Wheeler-Kenyon method
   (vertical archaeology)
Yigael Yadin

Further Reading

Cline, Eric H. *Biblical Archaeology: A Very Short Introduction.* Oxford: Oxford University Press, 2009.

Currid, John D. *Doing Archaeology in the Land of the Bible: A Basic Guide.* Grand Rapids: Baker, 1999.

White, Ellen, ed. *40 Futures: Experts Predict What's Next for Biblical Archaeology.* Digging Deeper 4. Washington, DC: Biblical Archaeology Society, 2015.

ENGAGING EXEGESIS

What Is *Exegesis*?

Exegesis is the basic method of interpretation used for biblical studies. The literal meaning of the word is "to lead" or "to guide out," and in this case it means to pull the meaning out of a text. In other words, exegesis is about determining the intended or proper meaning of a text. This is in opposition to *eisegesis*, which is reading something into the text that is foreign to it. When doing exegesis, even when using a method that focuses on the reader (rather than the author or the text), one must stay true to the spirit of the text and not introduce ideas or contexts that are contrary to it.[1]

When embarking on an exegesis, the interpreter is taking a journey through three worlds: the **world of the text** (the narrative world), the **world behind the text** (the author's world), and the **world in front of the text** (the reader's world). Each of these worlds affects one's interpretation of the text to a certain extent, depending on the hermeneutical—interpretive—method used. One's hermeneutical method often favors one of these three worlds over the others, but no method can (or should) be completely divorced from the others.[2] When doing biblical archaeology, the historical-critical method is

---

1. This chapter is greatly influenced by John L. McLaughlin's unpublished "Writing an Exegesis."

2. For a good explanation of the various methods used by contemporary scholars and the worlds to which they relate, see Corrine L. Carvalho, *Primer on Biblical Methods* (Winona, MN: Anselm Academic, 2009).

Worlds of the Text

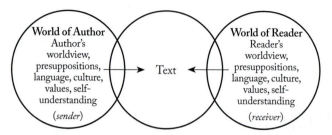

the most used because of its focus on the world behind the text (i.e., the world in which the author of the text lived); but here again the other two worlds must not be ignored, and other methods are sometimes helpful in examining particular questions that arise. Thus it is best not to imagine the interpreter as a slave to methodology but rather to imagine the interpretive methods as exegetical tools that can be used to explore the worlds belonging to the text.[3]

World of the Text

The world of the text is one that is created within the narrative and often differs from the author's and reader's worlds. Hogwarts, Narnia, Mordor, and the Seven Kingdoms are worlds of the text. The world of the text might mirror the world behind the text (i.e., the author's world) or it might depict something completely different. All literary elements combine to build the world of the text. Therefore, the **exegete** engages in a kind of literary archaeology by slowly and carefully removing each element and examining it to understand its relationship to the whole. Each piece matters. Whether it is a syntactical structure or a characterization, each rhetorical piece combines to draw the reader into the textual world. The world of the text is not limited by the rules of the author's reality and, therefore, can express desires, actions, and philosophies outside the norms of the world behind the text. It can be an imaginative world or even a revolutionary one. The world of the text is built on rhetorical rules rather than cultural ones.

---

3. For a detailed study on these worlds and the methods involved, as well as an integrated approach, see W. Randolph Tate, *Biblical Interpretation: An Integrated Approach* (Peabody, MA: Hendrickson, 2008).

Determine the Text

To begin an exegesis one must first determine the boundaries of the text. This may seem straightforward, but it isn't always and several factors are involved. Particularly important is that biblical chapter numbers cannot be used to decide this. The chapter and verse numbers that appear in a modern Bible are not part of the original text. The chapters were added in the thirteenth century and the verse numbers in the sixteenth century for the sake of convenient reference more than anything else. There are times when the chapters (and verses) may correspond to the beginning and end of a passage, but often this is not so. A good example appears in the opening chapters of Genesis, the first book of the Bible. Chapter 2 begins before the first creation narrative ends; in fact, at least the first three verses belong to the story in chapter 1. Further complicating the situation, the first creation narrative, Genesis 1:1–2:3, is followed by the second creation narrative, Genesis 2:5–25, but it is unclear whether verse 2:4 is the conclusion to the first creation narrative or the introduction to the second. The interpreter must address that issue when commencing study, and therefore must carefully read through the proposed text for clues to determine the limitations of the text.

Since the interpreter cannot simply rely upon the chapter and verse divisions in the text to determine a passage, other **literary features** must be used. Some of these features include structure, subdivisions, patterns, and **formulaic phrases**. The passage must form a logical and unified unit. Sometimes the division is obvious, such as the parameters of a poem. Most Psalms consist of one poem and therefore form a complete passage. There are some exceptions, such as Psalms 42 and 43, but since Hebrew poetry usually follows standard forms, recognizing exceptions should not prove too difficult. Outside of the Psalms, there are also certain introductory phrases, such as "Thus says the LORD" or "The word of the LORD came to him," that indicate a new textual unit is commencing. These phrases have a similar function to the use of **colophons**—markings at the end of the text that provide information about the publication and "catchphrases"—in Akkadian (another people group in the ANE) texts, but these colophons usually are found at the end of a text rather than at the beginning. Such markings were used to distinguish one type of text from another and to provide information regarding a text's composition. Like the formulaic phrases, they guide the reader's interpretation and understanding of the passage. Learning these phrases helps the exegete determine the proper beginning and end of a passage. A literary change of scene, time, or topic also signals the beginning of a new division (sometimes a subdivision in a longer narrative). These are all fairly familiar techniques for the modern reader as similar styles are still used by authors today.

Some literary features that might not be as readily apparent for a modern interpreter involve various **literary patterns** that were common when the Bible was written. One such feature is an *inclusio*, the repetition of words at the beginning and end of a literary unit (cf. Ps. 118:1, 29). An *inclusio* is similar to a chorus in music, except it is shorter and comes at both the beginning and end of a section. Other patterns found in the Bible might be familiar to a present-day reader, such as an acrostic. Used in poetry, an acrostic begins each line with a letter of the alphabet in sequential order (see the first four chapters of Lamentations). While this might not be new to readers today, it is not always apparent in an English translation since the alphabet of original composition is Hebrew.[4] Chiastic structure (sometimes called mirror pattern) is another common technique used in Scripture. Here the writer presents the narrative elements and then presents them again in reverse order (A, B, C, B', A'). A *chiasm* contains the same idea in the repetitions, but not necessarily verbatim. When there is a middle element that is without a pair, it is the author's way of highlighting and emphasizing that element. These structures can be large or small in scale. Other forms also exist, so it is important for an exegete to become familiar with these various textual clues to be certain of the parameters of the passage to be explored.

Another key consideration in establishing a passage is whether any additions have been made to the originally written text. This is important for two reasons: the first is that any additions likely come from a different world behind the text, which will affect how other interpretative tools are applied; the second is that an addition to a text may have altered the text's overall meaning (such alterations might demonstrate a theological development from the initial writing to the revision).

---

4. Not all acrostics are alphabet acrostics.

Textual changes and additions can happen for a number of reasons, both accidental and intentional. One way to determine if a text has been redacted—edited—is by comparing ancient manuscripts and searching for the most original version, what is called the *Ur-text*; none of these Ur-texts have been preserved as far as current research knows. Most New Testament translations are not based on a single manuscript, but are in fact a compilation of various witnesses (manuscripts) in an attempt to recreate the original—oldest—version. One of the rules that guides this textual criticism is the older a manuscript, the more valuable it is for reconstructing the original text.

The impact of these text progressions over time follows the same principle as the familiar game of "telephone," in which players form a line or circle and the first person in the line whispers a message to the ear of the next person, and so on down the line or around the circle until the last person receives the message and then recites it out loud to the group. Typically, in being passed along from ear to ear, the message becomes corrupted so that the first and last versions are markedly different. Sometimes players will even confess to changing elements, because what they received made no sense to them and they tried to correct it. A similar process happens to a text that is not mass produced and preserved, especially when communicated over centuries.

The discovery of ancient texts that contain early versions of the biblical books, such as the **Dead Sea Scrolls** (DSS), which date between 150 BCE and 70 CE, can help the interpreter see changes that may have been made in a passage. One example of this is Deuteronomy 32:8. Most translations, which are based on the **Masoretic Text** (MT), which comes from the tenth century CE, read this verse as saying God (*Elyon*) divided the people according to the "son of Israel." The DSS (4QDeut) text says they were divided according to "the sons of god."[5] The DSS text is significantly older than the MT and also more theologically difficult, and therefore, more likely original. A series of cuneiform tablets found in Ugarit (an ancient port city located in modern-day Syria) that are sometimes referred to as the Canaanite Bible (c. 1800–1200 BCE) and likely reflect the dominant theological position of the land that became Israel prior to its settlement, demonstrate that the chief god of the pantheon (divine government) was

---

5. This is also what is present in the Septuagint (abbreviated LXX), the Greek version of the Hebrew Bible.

sometimes referred to as Elyon and that the pantheon, or more simply the gods, were called "the sons of god." From these two versions of this verse, one might see a transition from polytheism toward monotheism. While this is a small **redaction** of only one word, it demonstrates the importance of recognizing textual changes or additions and the value of new literary finds regardless of size.

Understand the Genre

Genre is key to understanding a biblical text. *Genre* refers to the type of writing, and each style is governed by rules that are specific and unique to it. So much of a text's meaning is conveyed by its genre. Every genre contains specific elements to trigger the reader's understanding of a text. Once the reader knows what the genre is, the reader has an idea about how it should be understood.

Imagine for a moment the opening scene of a movie. The screen comes to life on a historic main street, with a dusty road, a tumbleweed rambling down the road. On one side of the road there is a saloon, its doors swinging back and forth with a slight creak. On the other side of the road stands a bank, a row of horses tied to a wooden post outside. The camera angle turns and shows either end of the street. At one end stands a man dressed in black, a bandana about his neck, his hands resting on the grips of two holstered guns; down the street stands another man, dressed in white and wearing a large-brimmed Stetson, a shotgun slung over his shoulder and a pistol within easy reach. Within seconds the audience understands this is a Western (the genre) and that they can expect a sheriff to suffer several setbacks and then ultimately defeat the villain and save the town (unless of course this Western has the classic genre twist of role reversal—i.e., the bad guy is actually the good guy—but even then, one can expect "the good" to win over "the bad").

Focusing on the exact wording of a passage does not mean reading the text literally, as this can lead to all kinds of problematic interpretations, because such a literal reading does not take genre into account. To change the genre of a narrative is to change the meaning of the text. Therefore, it is vital to establish the genre of a passage before attempting further exegesis. One should not read biblical law the same way as prophecy or apocalyptic literature, texts that have a hidden or symbolic meaning. The biblical text uses many forms (specific patterns that must be followed), and a reader must become familiar with them. For example, most of the Psalms follow one of four types that guide the elements contained within and the flow of the poetry. Prophetic call narratives (stories that detail how the prophet became a prophet) and miracle stories also share specific features that help the reader identify the genre, a necessary step toward gaining accurate insight into the author's or authors' theology.

Structure of Prophetic Call Narratives[6]

Narrative Element	Jeremiah	Isaiah
1. indication of need	1:3	6:1–2
2. commission	1:4–5	6:8–10
3. objection	1:6	6:11
4. assurance of support	1:8	6:11–13
5. signs	1:11–19	(absent)

Even though the overarching theme of the biblical text is theology—the study of God—the various independent genres present in the Bible serve this primary purpose in unique ways according to the rules that govern the genre of the specific passage.

Explore the Larger Context

A popular exegetical proverb states, "a text without context is pretext." Basically, this means any interpretation that doesn't consider the broader context of a passage is by nature going to fall short, be inadequate, or be wrong. For the Bible, the larger context boils down to three levels: words and phrases, the entire narrative or book (and potentially the whole canon), and the world behind the text.

---

6. The classical study of prophetic call narratives is Norman Habel, "The Form and Significance of the Call Narratives," *Zeitschrift für die alttestamentliche Wissenschaft* 77 (1965): 298. I have not differed from the divisions given there.

What does it mean to explore the broader context of a word or phrase? Don't words just mean what they mean? Sure, but many, if not most, words have multiple meanings. A native reader often instinctively understands the intended meaning based on repeated exposure to the word; this is the context of the word for that reader. Scholars refer to these multiple meanings as the **semantic range** of the word. Take, for example, the English word *well*. Ponder the following sentence: Well, she would do well to go get water from the well and see if the bucket is functioning well, while she is still feeling well. Despite being a horribly ugly English sentence, it uses the word *well* in five different ways, but the overall meaning is still clear: *[Interjection]*, it would be *good* for her to get water from the *intentional hole in the ground* so she can see if the bucket *is functioning*, while she is still feeling *healthy*. The range of meanings here is diverse and one cannot substitute a single different word to replace each instance of *well*. Likely this would still hold true if the sentence were translated to another language. In German, for example, each instance of *well* would be replaced by a completely different word: not translatable, *gut, der Brunnen, funkionert, gesund.*

A word's semantic range is unique to the language in which it is written; therefore, it is important to do a **word study** of key terms found in a biblical passage. For such a word study, the interpreter looks up every instance of a word in the Bible. Concordances, which provide lists of every word in the Bible and where it appears, and specialized computer programs are useful for this; lexicons, dictionaries of Greek, Hebrew, and Aramaic, can also be helpful in this process. The interpreter then examines the use of the word in each of these various contexts. For particular or rare words, it can be helpful to explore more texts that arise from the same world. For example, Genesis 2:18 states that the human (usually translated as man) should not be alone and that God will make it a "helper." This word has been used to legitimize the subjugation of women to men for centuries in the English-speaking world. This is probably because in English the "helper" is secondary to the one being helped, and so it was understood that women were created to perform a secondary role to men. Yet a word study of this term will demonstrate that usually when it is used in the Bible it refers to God as the "helper" (cf. Exod. 18:4; Deut. 33:7, 26, 29; Ps. 33:20; 115:9–11; 121:2; 124:8; 146:5), and there is absolutely no subservience indicated. This example demonstrates how important it is to understand each word in context so as not to misinterpret the specific passage.

In addition to looking within the text of the Bible, scholars often include other ancient texts written in the same language or in cognate languages (languages having a common linguistic background). Many of these additional texts are the result of archaeological excavation in the geographical region associated with the Bible, and although they might have no connection to the Bible, such as a Babylonian administrative text, they still have value to biblical scholars because the texts provide scholars with more linguistic data that can help form their interpretations.

The larger **textual context** is also necessary to understand specific passages. While one's textual unit might be well established, it is still one part of the larger whole, and there is an expectation that the unit fits within that larger work and somehow contributes to its overall message. Sometimes knowledge of the overarching themes of a book are important for interpreting an individual passage. Take the Gospel of Mark, for example. In Mark 1:21–2:12 Jesus is engaged in various healings. These are done in public and cause Jesus to develop quite a reputation. In this section it appears that Jesus is trying to garner the attention of Galilee and that his main attention-getting strategy is through healings and exorcism. Yet in the middle of this passage (1:40–45), Jesus heals a leper and then tells him to "say nothing to anyone." This instruction, which the leper does not follow, makes no sense in the context of this subsection. Yet within the Gospel of Mark as a whole, it fits an overarching theme known as the Messianic Secret (a collection of verses designed to hide Jesus' identity as the Messiah). This secret is a distinctive characteristic of Mark and thus likely presents an important element of Markan theology, though what that might be is still hotly contested among scholars. Thus it is vital that exegetes not only explore their passage in depth but also in breadth.

World behind the Text

The world behind the text is the world in which the text was written—that is, the author's world. This world has a specific historic location with rules and expectations that are particular to that place and time. This is the world that archaeologists are exploring. The world behind the text is the living context of the author(s). It is the author's unique world that has been developed through that author's experiences. Sometimes the author and social setting for a particular text is known, even a text from long ago. For example, it is known that Geoffrey Chaucer was the author of the *Canterbury Tales* and that it was written in fourteenth-century London, England. When both the author and historical location of a text are known, it is much easier for a scholar to access the world behind the text.

There are times when the historical location of a text is known but the author is not, or perhaps the identity of the author is unclear. The classic English poem *Beowulf* provides a good example of this. Written at the end of the eighth or early ninth century, *Beowulf* is set in Scandinavia (the world of the text) and written in Old English, most likely by an Anglo-Saxon. Knowing the historical setting for the poem can help with its interpretation, but lack of knowledge about the author limits one's understanding the world behind the text.

Pseudonymous texts—that is, those composed under a false name—can be equally problematic for this reason. Authors might hide their identity for several reasons, such as gender or sociopolitical concerns. Mary Ann Evans, who adopted the name George Eliot when she published *Middlemarch*, was an example of the former. She used a masculine pen name because she wanted her work taken seriously—the stereotype at the time was that female authors wrote fluff and romance—and to distance her public writing from her private life. For sociopolitical reasons, some argue that the actual author of the works of Shakespeare was a well-respected public figure rather than the bard from humble beginnings, and that this respected lawyer or politician—depending on the theory—didn't want the association with theater, a less reputable profession at the time, to damage his reputation. Yet other authors use a pseudonym as homage to the one whose name they adopt; this is often the case with ancient texts. In the Bible, for example, several books are ascribed to King Solomon because he was considered the wisest man to ever live, and therefore the book would also be considered wise.

Other ancient texts have no specified historical location or author and, therefore, scholars need to engage in detective-like investigations to discover the world behind the text. While scholars diligently attempt to find this world, sometimes the location remains elusive or the investigations lead to multiple possibilities. The biblical book of Job, for example, wrestles with the question of why bad things happen to good—and in this case godly—people. Many conjecture this biblical book was written as a response to the Babylonian Exile—the captivity of the Jews in Babylon from 598/7 to 538 BCE following mass deportations that occurred after the Babylonian Empire conquered Judah[7]—because of the suffering of the righteous. This is not definitive, however, because humans have been attempting to explain such injustice throughout history (and still today). Some have tried to date this text based on the linguistic evidence—language and writing style changes over time—but this too has mixed results. There are also comparable texts from the ancient Near East with clearer composition dates that are sometimes used to try to determine the origin of Job, but this too fails attempt as this is a dominant literary theme in the region for centuries.

Historical Setting

Having knowledge of the world behind the text is key to understanding the historical setting of the work. Modern readers or consumers of television know the most common literary setting is the author's own world. The story, play, or novel usually takes place in a world contemporaneous to the author with many of the elements of contemporary life woven into the plot (often unintentionally).

To illustrate with a contemporary example, it is clear that Superman was not written in the era of cell phones, as Clark Kent would have needed somewhere other than a phone booth to make his transformation. Here the authors were not trying to make a point about communication patterns or an apologetic for antiquated technology, but rather Jerry Siegel and Joe Shuster merely adopted an object that

---

7. The name *Israel* is complicated in the Bible. Originally, the name belonged to one man, Jacob, who was given this new name by God. During the time of the Judges, Israel referred to a loose federation of tribes, and later it was the name of the nation during the United Monarchy (the reigns of Saul, David, and Solomon). After the civil war, the Northern Kingdom adopted the name Israel (the Southern Kingdom was called Judah), but it was destroyed by the Assyrians in 722 BCE. When the Jewish exiles returned from captivity in Babylon, they took the name Israel, despite all originating from Judah.

was part of their everyday world that would serve their literary purpose, which was to allow Clark Kent to become Superman while in public. The interpreter must determine which elements are relevant and which are merely representative.

In the Bible, this is seen in many places, and the interpreter must determine if the object itself is significant or is an everyday item used to further the author's theological point. One example of this can be found in both Isaiah 2:4 and Micah 4:3, which contain the prophecy that they shall beat their "swords into plowshares."[8] Perhaps modern readers of these texts are unfamiliar with plowshares, especially urbanites, but in the mainly agrarian society of Israel, these ground-tilling blades were common. The plowshares themselves are not important; they are only used to serve the message. Here the prophets are saying, trust God for protection (not their own swords) and use metal resources for useful survival tools. The biblical scholar is interested in the type of work that should be left to God (protection services) and the type of work for which human beings are responsible (working the land),[9] whereas the archaeologist would be interested in the items (sword and plowshare) and the process that would be available to the Israelites for transforming one item into the other. The objects of interest might be the same, but the realm of interpretation has different focuses.

If something is not historically accurate, then the author is most likely using it to make a point, and the inauthenticity is a clue for the reader; however, when something is authentic, then it becomes more difficult for the reader to determine its purpose in the text. For example, in Genesis 3 a serpent comes to the first couple, Adam and Eve, and discusses whether they should eat from the Tree of Knowledge. The appearance of a serpent in a garden in that part of the world is nothing out of the ordinary. Many readers will never question why it is a serpent that approaches the couple rather than a gazelle or a bird. Yet in this case the seemingly representative element is, in fact, relevant. The choice of the serpent is interpretive. Throughout the

---

8. Interestingly, this phrase is reversed in Joel 3:10, as the author of Joel is writing to a different context with a different theological agenda.

9. This theme can be seen elsewhere in the biblical text, including when the first couple is expelled from the Garden of Eden.

ANE, serpents represent wisdom, and thus it is the right choice from the animal kingdom to engage in a theological conversation with the ultimate creatures of creation. This is not easy to see from the text alone, but paired with other biblical and ANE texts, along with the iconography of the ANE, this simple element is revealed to have a deeper purpose and to affect the reader's interpretation.

Ironically, the biblical scholar often is more interested in the ahistorical elements in the text, whereas the archaeologist wants to further examine the historical elements. In the Superman example, the exegete would ignore the phone booth and focus on Kent changing to hide his identity, but the archaeologist would want to know every detail about the booth itself. Thus readers must familiarize themselves with the historical background of a text to distinguish between the normal from the abnormal.

Other times, the use of the author's world is intentional. Late night talk-show monologues are a good example of writing that intentionally weaves current historical events into the script. In these monologues, the host names real people and events and uses humor to make a point about current events—usually as humorous critique. In this way the comedians' intentional use of their historical context mirrors that of the prophets, who also use dramatic means to attract audiences (e.g., Isaiah spent three years of his prophecy naked) and to draw attention to their messages.

Sometimes the use of the author's world is allegorical and intended to provide societal commentary. For example, Susanne Collins' trilogy, *The Hunger Games*, is an allegory for society's obsession with reality television, and the classic Dr. Seuss story *Yertle the Turtle* (meant to symbolize Adolf Hitler) warns against the evils of totalitarianism. Yet to understand the commentary within the allegory (the moral of the story) one must first understand the historical event or phenomenon the author is commenting on. Allegory is not that different from the genres of apocalyptic literature or parable, all of which contain symbolic meanings.

Sociocultural Presuppositions

Understanding the world behind the text is more than just familiarizing oneself with the historical events and figures at the time the text was recorded. Every culture has its own set of presuppositions, and often the residents of a society are not even conscious of the presuppositions they operate under; all of this is just "the way things are." Sometimes these presuppositions are the ingrained "truths" the society holds to be self-evident, and other times the people themselves may no longer even know or understand the reasons for their traditions and beliefs.

It is like that old joke about the newlywed couple. The husband wants to cook a roast for his wife just like the roasts his mother and grandmother used to make for his family growing up. So he brings home a beautiful side of beef and proceeds to cut the end from it. His wife exclaims, "What are you doing!? That is good meat." He replies, "No! You are supposed to cut the end off and throw it away!" They bicker back and forth for a while until finally, in a fit of frustration, the husband exclaims, "I am calling my mother!" Once his mother is on the phone (on speaker of course), she confirms the end of the beef should be removed and discarded, but the wife still insists this is a crazy waste. Eventually, it is decided to conference grandma into the call. Grandma listens carefully to the concern. Then she says, "No, you do not have to cut the end of the meat off, I always did because the roasts the local butcher sold were just slightly bigger than my roasting pan." The exegete must return to the grandmother of the text, and not assume that the husband of the text knows why he is doing what he is doing or that his reasoning is the same as the initial reason. Ritual practices are particularly prone to presuppositions, and the biblical texts refer to many ritual practices.

A biblical example of this can be difficult to interpret. Assessing whether the characters are aware of the origin for their own actions is an interpretive action. A good example of this can be found in Ruth 4:7. In Ruth 4, Boaz approaches a senior relative (SR) regarding a plot of land that Naomi (a distant relative of both) has for sale since, as the oldest male relative, the SR has first right of refusal. The SR initially agrees to buy the land until he learns that it comes with Ruth's (Naomi's daughter-in-law) hand in marriage, and then he declines. At that point Boaz says he will purchase the land and marry Ruth and proceeds to hand the SR his shoe in front of elders at the town gates (witnesses). Verse 7 states that ancient custom dictates that when a deal is struck, one party removes his shoe and presents it to the other and this is what legalizes the contract. The presence of this verse explaining the ritual implies the reader would no longer be familiar with the custom, but it might also imply that Boaz himself did not understand the reason behind his offering of the shoe, especially since he emphasizes the presence of the witnesses for the legality of the transaction. Here Boaz follows ancient legal ritual, but it is unclear whether he understands the significance of that ritual. Exploring these questions is part of the interpretive task.

Presuppositions also reflect the social rules of a culture. For example, in ancient Israel it was expected that the firstborn son would inherit the family assets; this practice is called *primogeniture*. Primogeniture was not merely an occasional or even a frequent practice—it was the expected norm from which one did not deviate. Therefore, it is reasonable to expect that this hard and fast societal rule would be upheld in the biblical text. But it is not. In fact, one frequently sees the reversal of primogeniture with respect to the line of promise. In every generation following Abraham in Genesis, this unexpected reversal occurs: Ishmael not Isaac is the firstborn, yet Isaac is the chosen son of promise; Esau not Jacob is the firstborn, yet Jacob is the one God chooses; Reuben not Judah is the firstborn, and yet Judah receives the blessing and enters the line of promise. This total violation of the accepted sociocultural regulations can only be intentional and, therefore, must be examined further for theological significance.[10] Yet, without knowledge of the world behind the text, a modern reader might think nothing of later-born children inheriting. One must become acquainted with the culture of the world behind the text to locate the meaning within the text.

Theological Background

There are times when modern readers will struggle to remove the Bible from its current **theological context**. This privileging of the present moment makes it difficult to read certain texts in the spirit in which they were written. The theological background of the texts is radically different from the theological landscape of today. Just

---

10. For a good discussion of the various understandings of this reversal, see Roger Syren, *The Forsaken First-Born: A Study of a Recurrent Motif in the Patriarchal Narratives*, JSOTSS 133 (Sheffield: Sheffield Academic Press, 1993).

imagine a world without Christianity and the difference that would make for society and politics within the community, state, country, and the world. Add to that a setting without Judaism or Islam. The dominant perspectives on theology during biblical times are radically different from those that permeate the contemporary reader's world.

In the contemporary Western world, for example, God's presence does not have a specific location. In the ancient world, however, each land had a specific god that was associated with that land's very ground—and gods did not relocate. The story of Naaman (2 Kings 5) demonstrates this when, after a miraculous healing, Naaman, an Assyrian commander, converts to Yahweh worship. When he returns to his home, he takes as much earth from Israel "as two mules can carry." He transports the actual ground in order to be able to worship Yahweh. This seemingly minor detail in this narrative actually reveals a pervasive belief in the ancient world and is one of the reasons why the Babylonian Exile was a major theological crisis for Israel. Suddenly, the Israelites found themselves outside of the land of Yahweh and living in the land of Marduk. Does this mean the Israelites believed Marduk to be mightier than Yahweh? Did they feel compelled to convert? Many biblical texts and the religious traditions that developed from them aim to provide answers for this theological crisis. Without understanding the theological consensus of the time, one does not understand the revolutionary nature of the texts. The texts that deal with the Exile are not merely factual retellings, but a historiographic apologetic to persuade the readers to accept their theology. Just as it is important to study the laws and customs that were prevalent at the time, understanding the theological background, within Israel, its neighbors, and its enemies, is essential.

Ancient Parallels

A common phenomenon these days is for American television and film producers to remake slightly older British shows, such as *The Office*, *House of Cards*, and *Being Human*. The American show follows the pattern of the British show and often involves the same characters, but they are not quite the same. Certain changes are made to adapt to culture and fill different nuances of need. Overall, the shows service the same desires in viewers—satirical humor regarding the drudgery of office life; dark, skeptical political commentary; and lighthearted, angsty teen fantasy. One can become an expert on the new version by watching it many times, engaging in discussions in the blogosphere, and even attending conferences dedicated to the show's fandom and still not gain the insight and perspective that can be found by also studying the older version.

While this analogy is imperfect, the comparison helps one understand why ancient texts that parallel and originate from the same region as a biblical text are important in biblical exegesis. For example, there are many ancient flood narratives—stories that refer to a catastrophic flood—but the Bible is unique in the reason it provides for the flood. Genesis 6–9 contains the story of Noah and a worldwide flood. In this story, the narrator explains that

Jack1956 / Wikimedia / Bm-epic-g.jpg / CC0

due to the overwhelming wickedness found in the world, God has no choice but to destroy the world by flood, saving only Noah, his family, and a representative sampling of animals on a large boat that God instructed Noah to build. First uncovered in the Nineveh excavations, the *Epic of Atrahasis* is an eighteenth-century BCE Akkadian text that was first rediscovered in the library of Ashurbanipal. Tablet III contains a flood narrative that shares many similarities with the biblical narrative, but also important differences. In this version, Atrahasis (whose name means "extremely wise") is warned by one of the gods about a coming worldwide

The Epic of Atrahasis, currently housed in the British Museum, contains an eighteenth century BCE Akkadian flood narrative. While it bears many similarities to the biblical flood narrative, the reason for the destruction of humankind is divergent. In the biblical story, humans must be destroyed because their sins are irredeemable; in the Akkadian, the humans were noisy and annoyed the gods. This difference demonstrates the uniqueness of Israelite theology.

flood and is instructed to build a boat to survive. Key differences are the presence of multiple gods and the reason for the flood: the gods found humans to be too noisy. In the Bible, God, in order to be just, is shown to have no other option but to destroy humanity due to extreme wickedness; but in the *Epic of Atrahasis*, the gods are malevolent beings who punish a minor infraction with capital punishment. The theological insight gained through this comparison highlights the extreme opposite understanding of god(s). Noting the differences between the biblical text and the **ancient parallels** can help highlight the purpose of the biblical passage. By comparing parallels, one can illuminate the specific theological insights of the Bible.

Genre provides yet another point of comparison between biblical texts and some of their ancient precursors. In ancient biography, for example, one finds a striking parallel to the biblical accounts of Jesus. In Philostratus's *Life of Apollonius*, the events in the life of Apollonius of Tyana mirror many aspects of the life of Jesus.[11] Apollonius's birth was announced to his mother by a divine being and his birth was accompanied by supernatural signs. He was said to be divine and a spiritual authority (from childhood). An itinerant preacher who had disciples, Apollonius could perform miracles, such as healing the sick and raising the dead. He was tried and put to death by the Romans, but he appeared to his followers after his death and ascended into heaven. Finally, stories about his life were later written down by his followers. For anyone familiar with the Gospel narratives, this will sound eerily similar to the story of Jesus. In fact, if you asked the average person sitting in a church pew to tell you about Jesus, these are probably the things the individual would say. Yet what if these elements are merely part of the genre? Just as a fictional horse, pistol, saloon girl, and tumbleweed are meant to tell a reader that the story is a Western, so the supernatural birth and identity, miracles, and triumph over death are meant to signal to the reader that the genre is

---

11. For full details and how this applies to New Testament interpretation, see Bart D. Ehrman, *The New Testament: A Historical Introduction to the Early Christian Writings* (New York: Oxford University Press, 2004), 18–23. Philostratus was writing about 220 CE, which raises an important question in the handling of parallels: which version is influencing which? Were the Gospel accounts of Jesus influenced by works like Philostratus's, or was the depiction of Apollonius influenced by the Gospel accounts, or is it some combination of the two? In this instance, influential direction is a matter of great debate, but for the previous example, the *Epic of Atrahasis* predates the writing of Genesis by many centuries and, therefore, must be the source of any influence.

an ancient biography of a particular type of figure (son of god, philosopher, emperor, etc.). This leaves one to wonder about the point of the Gospel narratives. The answer serves to explain why there are four of them. Once the interpreter strips away these identical elements in the Jesus of the Gospels, the unique perspective of each writer comes out.[12] For example, Matthew has a Jewish focus and places emphasis on the Kingdom of Heaven, whereas Luke is focused on Gentiles and interpersonal relationships. Since uniqueness is located in difference, comparative analysis allows the interpreter to better access the distinctive points of the biblical authors.

World in Front of the Text

The world in front of the text belongs to the reader. The text needs the reader in a practical sense; if a text is not read, it has no function or meaning. The reader is the one who ultimately determines the meaning of a text, and that determination is based on the reader's context. Just as authors are products of their environments, so too are readers, and readers bring those contexts and their **preconceptions** to what they read. Often texts require the reader to fill in missing information. Sometimes the missing information is unstated cultural norms that can be learned from studying the world behind the text. Other times such norms are missing and can only be provided by the reader.

Take the story about Joseph and Potiphar's wife in Genesis 39, for example. In this story, Joseph has been sold into slavery by his brothers. He is purchased by Potiphar, the captain of Pharaoh's guards. Potiphar quickly realizes that Joseph is intelligent and capable and so trusts him with overseeing his household. Potiphar's wife, however, notices Joseph is very sexually attractive and she attempts to seduce him. When Joseph refuses her, she lies and claims he has tried to sexually assault her. As a result, Joseph is thrown in jail. Many sermons have been written about the great virtue of Joseph and the amazing restraint he shows in refusing the persistent seductions of this woman, and Joseph himself states that it would be a great sin to give in (v. 9).

---

12. This is not to say that there is no theological value in these shared elements and, in fact, further comparative analysis could serve to demonstrate unique features and ideas woven into these elements as well, so they are not to be merely discarded.

Yet while the text states Joseph is very handsome, it says nothing about Potiphar's wife. These virtuous interpretations about Joseph assume he is rejecting something appealing. The text is silent about whether this woman is desirable; it is also silent about Joseph's virtue in this situation and gives him no praise for his refusal. Imagine how different the interpretation might be if the reader pictures a much older, ugly woman coming on to this young stud. The reality is it is not the text that determines the interpretation here, it is the reader's imagination. By nature of a human brain, readers must fill in these gaps to formulate the picture in their minds. As different readers fill in these gaps differently, various interpretations of a single text become possible, even likely.

The reader's context often determines the questions the interpreter asks of a given text and the way the interpreter understands it. These questions will differ among readers based on many factors, including gender, race, culture, age, education, religion, social status, and so on. A person's various identities place one within certain **reading communities,** and it is from within these communities that certain **hermeneutics**—the intersection between the original meaning and the modern setting—develop. It is possible to understand biblical archaeology as a reading community. Those engaged in biblical archaeology share a common set of assumptions (e.g., archaeology is relevant to biblical interpretation), and yet the practice of it can reveal other preconceptions that practitioners hold from their membership in other reading communities.

While hermeneutics have always played a role in biblical exegesis, a new emphasis awakened in the 1970s that recognized a neutral or plain reading of a text was almost impossible to achieve and that readings touted as such were really just reflections of the primary reading community (dominantly Western-educated Caucasian males). The goal of modern hermeneutics is not to compete with other reading communities' experiential readings but rather to diversify the number of experiences involved in interpretation—modern hermeneutics is about expanding rather than restricting. Biblical scholar W. Randolph Tate summarizes this well: "Reading is dynamic, open-ended, always subject to modification, change, evaluation, and rereading."[13]

---

13. Tate, *Biblical Interpretation,* 192.

Applications

Many engage in exegesis to teach the text in a faith community or to preach from it. If that is one's goal, then one must address how to properly apply the passage to contemporary times. In other words, what are the implications of exegesis for today? This must, however, be the final step in any exegetical endeavor, because the application must be rooted in the discovered meaning(s) of the text; otherwise, the text once again loses its context and becomes pretext. Application is not about how a text makes one feel but rather the interpreted meaning uncovered after careful study. There are good interpretations and bad interpretations, and thus there are good applications and bad applications; this is not a situation in which everyone's opinion is equal. Because the Bible is a text that greatly influences three major faith traditions, exegesis is not purely an academic exercise, as it has ramifications for a large number of believers, and thus it is imperative that such exegesis is done correctly, critically, and respectfully.

Questions for Review and Discussion

1. What are the main differences among the three textual worlds?
2. Do you think that one of the textual worlds is more important than the others for biblical interpretation? Explain your answer.
3. Can you see ways in which the world of the text or the world behind the text can be used to evaluate one's interpretation of a passage?
4. Which textual world do you think is most important for archaeology and why? How might the other two worlds be of value for the archaeologist?

Key Terms

ancient parallels
colophons
Dead Sea Scrolls
exegesis

exegete
formulaic phrase
genre
hermeneutics

continued

Key Terms *continued*

literary features
literary patterns (inclusio,
    chiasm, acrostic)
Masoretic Text
preconceptions
pseudonymous texts
reading communities
redaction

semantic range
textual context
theological context
word study
world behind the text
world in front of the text
world of the text

Further Reading

Camery-Hoggatt, Jerry. *Reading the Good Book Well: A Guide to Biblical Interpretation*. Nashville: Abingdon, 2007.

Carvalho, Corrine L. *Primer on Biblical Methods*. Winona, MN: Anselm Academic, 2009.

McKenzie, Steven L. *How to Read the Bible: History, Prophecy, Literature—Why Modern Readers Need to Know the Difference and What It Means for Faith Today*. New York: Oxford University Press, 2005.

Tate, W. Randolph. *Biblical Interpretation: An Integrated Approach*. Peabody, MA: Hendrickson, 2008.

BIBLICAL EXEGESIS AND ARCHAEOLOGY: STRONGER TOGETHER

B iblical archaeology is essentially the **dialogue** between biblical studies and archaeology. Biblical archaeology results from these two fields merging to answer an interpretive question. The questions vary, but all have a historical aspect. Biblical archaeology is interested in history during the biblical period that can shed light on the Bible's interpretation and ultimately its hermeneutics, the various lenses through which the Bible is viewed and understood. Biblical archaeology explores the theological text of the Bible for historical elements and the material remains of archaeology for their theological elements. Both data sets come together to help the researcher better understand the whole. While some may assume a unidirectional relationship (archaeology enlightening the biblical texts or vice versa), this is not the case.

Many archaeological finds are challenging to understand, even when found in **context** (that is, in their original setting). For example, throughout modern-day Israel, archaeologists have found female **pillar figurines**. These figures have large bosoms and pelvises, but tree trunks in place of legs; they are often found in residential buildings but also sometimes in cultic sites. What are these figurines and what was their function? Are they an ancient version of a Barbie doll? Some kind of holiday decoration or dinner table centerpiece? A religious icon? The prevalence of them across the land and in multiple contexts makes this a difficult question to answer. Yet biblical passages that were written in or describe a contemporaneous time can shed light on this widespread phenomenon.

Genesis 31 describes a story in which one of the founding mothers, Rachel, steals the **household gods** of her father, Laban, before moving with her husband, Jacob, to Canaan. When Laban chases after them to regain his household gods (he assumes Jacob has stolen them), Rachel hides them in a saddle that she sits on. This implies two things: (1) household gods are small enough to hide by sitting on them, and (2) the ancients kept household gods in their homes. Because the size and context fits, the pillar figurines are perhaps household gods—that is, they are icons serving to represent a deity.

The Metropolitan Museum of Art, Gift of Harris D. and H. Dunscombe Colt, 1934

Female pillar figurines, characterized by over-emphasized female parts and bases like tree trunks, are prevalent in ancient Israelite sites. Scholars continue to debate the meaning and purpose of the figurines.

This conjecture, even if true, still doesn't answer every question about the pillar figurines, the most obvious being, which god is represented? The Bible can be helpful here too. There are several options in the ancient Near East for goddesses, but one fits the context best: Asherah. According to the Bible, Asherah was worshipped throughout Israel, which is why in the books of Kings there are regular pronouncements against her (one does not have to repeatedly tell people not to worship something they are not worshipping). This establishes that Asherah worship was prevalent in the land where the female pillar figurines were found. Second, the pillar figurines usually are supported by a tree trunk, and again the Bible describes her cultic symbol as a tree (cf. Exod. 34:13; Deut. 16:21; Judg. 6:25–27; 1 Kings 14:23; 2 Kings 21:7; 23:14).

A cultic figure is a regular item that represents a god;[1] a familiar later example is the fish symbol used to represent Christ. Additionally, from the cuneiform tablets found at Ugarit, it is known that Asherah[2] is the mother of the gods, and this would account for the extreme fertility features on the figurines. In this example, the texts help explain the archaeological data and thus lead to a fuller interpretation.

The Origins of Ancient Israel

There are other times when archaeology and biblical studies ask the same questions. A best possible answer considers evidence from both biblical studies and archaeology—that is, from biblical archaeology.

One of the most debated issues in biblical archaeology is how the nation of Israel developed.[3] In other words, who were the Israelites before they were Israelites and where did they come from before arriving in Canaan? Such questions might seem surprising, especially given the well-known biblical claim that the descendants of Abraham ended up in Egypt and over the centuries became slaves who, with God's help, escaped Egypt in miraculous numbers, took over the promised land (i.e., Canaan), and settled it. Yet even a simple biblical reading demonstrates much more complexity, so the questions remain unanswered.

Over the years, many proposals have attempted to answer the debate over the origins of Israel, but the theories usually fall into one of three models. Each of these models is a good example of biblical archaeology (regardless of which, if any, is correct). Each model has

---

1. This is an interpretation and not all scholars concur with this conclusion (though it is probably the dominant theory at the time of writing). Archaeologist Erin Darby, in her extensive study, argues that the base of these figurines is merely a base to support the weight of the statute and not meant to represent a tree trunk; *Interpreting Judean Pillar Figurines: Gender and Empire in Judean Apotropaic Ritual*, FAT II 69 (Tübingen: Mohr Siebeck, 2014), 311. She also questions their identification as goddess symbols (399). With further time, reflection, and discoveries, Darby's position that the figurines are used for protection and healing without any divine association could become the dominant scholarly position (404). This is the reason for continual reinterpretation.

2. As with many things in academia, not all scholars agree with this particular interpretation and propose other options, such as Astarte.

3. Special thanks and acknowledgment to John L. McLaughlin, who helped me frame these theories in this way.

biblical and archaeological arguments both for and against them. By marrying these two data sets (the Bible and archaeology), theorists are acting as biblical archaeologists, and their responses represent critical biblical archaeology.

The purpose of the exploration that follows is to see how biblical archaeology is conducted and the type of results it generates, not to establish a definitive answer to the question of Israel's origin. A definitive proposal has not yet been made, and more biblical archaeology is needed to determine who the Israelites were and how they came to live in the land. Biblical scholarship and archaeology are not static fields, and with new data and interpretations, new dialogues must occur. Rarely does biblical archaeology result in firm conclusions, but it does help weed out faulty theories and provide fuller understanding of the questions asked by biblical scholars and archaeologists.

The Conquest Model for the Origins of Israel

The **conquest model**, championed by Albright, envisions a mass exodus from Egypt, with all the Israelites coming as a pre-formed people group into the land. After a rapid succession of wars, the Israelites conquer the land and leave no survivors.

Biblical Arguments in Favor of the Conquest Model

The biblical arguments in favor of this model come from the book of Joshua. This biblical book depicts Joshua leading the Israelites into the promised land, quickly conquering the various (and usually more powerful) nations that live there, before settling in the land themselves. The text describes how Joshua purges the land, beginning with the supernatural collapse of the walls around Jericho and then moves on to victories against Ai, Hebron, Jarmuth, Lachish, and Eglon. Finally, Joshua miraculously manages to make the sun stand still to gain victory over Gibeon, which only serves to highlight the rapid pace of the text. That might sound like a contradiction (slowing down time as evidence of speed), but the miraculous action was taken to ensure the battle was concluded that day and not extended—this campaign was not to drag on.

Archaeological Arguments in Favor of the Conquest Model

Cities such as Lachish, Eglon, Debir, Bethel, and Hazor show evidence of destruction at an appropriate level of strata, which could indicate the Israelites battled these cities. In Hazor, there are remains of a simpler resettlement on the site, which one would expect from the conquest model.

Beginning in the late thirteenth century, around three hundred small agricultural villages appear in the central highlands, stretching from the hills in Galilee to the region around Beersheba. During this period, the population rose from about twelve thousand to about fifty-five thousand, an increase that cannot be explained by natural means or by small groups of nomads settling down. This suggests instead that a large number of people arrived in the region from outside the land and settled a previously underpopulated area outside the major Canaanite urban centers. Within these settlements, the major form of architecture was the four-room house. While this type of dwelling served an agrarian village well, it was unknown in the large Canaanite cities and appears to have been developed for these villages. In addition, these settlements used new or previously rare forms of terracing (a type of farming that levels slices of the hillside), plastered cisterns, and stone-lined silos.

© Bill Schlegel / BiblePlaces.com

Four-room houses, like this one at Hazor, were common among the people who would become the Israelites. The four sections were not always walled off. Other common features included an open-air courtyard, sleeping quarters on an upper story, and placement adjoining the houses beside them or the city's defensive wall.

Most of the pottery remains the same (LB II), but some hand-thrown wares appear (rather than those produced on a fast wheel).

Biblical Arguments against the Conquest Model

The book of Joshua consists of two parts. The first describes the Israelites' tsunami of war to overtake the land, and the second recounts Joshua's division of the land among the tribes. In this second section, the area of land divided is much larger than that conquered in the previous section. The book of Joshua describes no victories over the coastal plains (easily the most valuable landmass in the region), the central hill country, or major cities in the Jezreel Valley. There are, however, references to undefeated enemies (13:26; 15:63; 16:10; 17:11–13; 16–18). The first half of Joshua makes a theological point about the might of Israel's god and therefore presents an overwhelming and decisive military campaign; however, the theological point in the second half shifts slightly and details the division of the land among the tribes, with several indications that it had not been emptied by the Israelites. There is a well-established principle in biblical studies called "**reading against the grain**." When one reads against the grain, one looks for elements that seem contradictory to the main point of the author(s) and regards such counterpoints as more likely historical, because an author is more likely to include a detail that contradicts the author's message if that detail is true (or, in other words, an author is unlikely to make up a detail that contradicts the author's purpose or message).

The conquest model views the Israelites as a smaller, weaker nation that can conquer other nations only with supernatural help from their god (and by carefully obeying all of this god's wartime instructions). Yet, if the number of Israelites presented in Exodus 12:37 was historically accurate for the time described, the Israelites would have significantly outnumbered the Egyptian army, the major superpower of the time, and could easily have overpowered them (especially if they had been engaged in the type of grueling manual labor recounted in the texts, since that would make them extremely physically fit). However, the numbers presented in Exodus seem plausible (based on archaeology) for the period of the monarchy (c. 1030–931 BCE), and thus the author(s) may have read these early nation figures back into their origins.

Finally, the most challenging biblical evidence against the conquest model is the book of Judges. In this book, the Israelites are a sometimes-united coalition of tribes that regularly battle the surrounding people of the land (thus demonstrating they were not utterly destroyed as described in Joshua) and even each other (see Judg. 9; 19; 21). Judges presents a people who are struggling to maintain their foothold in a region filled with enemies. There are other contradictions between Joshua and Judges. For example, Joshua 10:36 claims that Joshua conquered Hebron, but Judges 1:10 gives the same victory over Hebron to the tribe of Judah at a later time. Additionally, Joshua 11 presents a military campaign in the north, but this radically differs from the presentation of the same conquest in Judges 4. The dominance of the theological historiography of the Bible can make it difficult to determine the history of the Late Bronze Age (1550–1200 BCE) from the biblical text.

Archaeological Arguments against the Conquest Model

The book of Joshua gives the impression that the Israelites' conquest of the land took between a year and a half to three years to complete; however, the destruction layers at archaeological sites containing evidence of conflict in this area span more than a one-hundred-year period, so if this destruction was caused by the Israelites, then this would indicate a gradual overtaking of the region, not a blitzkrieg. Similarly, although the city of Hazor was destroyed and resettled, the resettlement did not occur until 150 years later, and this does not fit with the conquest theory. Furthermore, several of the sites, such as Jericho, Ai, Gibeon, and Arad, all of which play a prominent role in Joshua, show no evidence of settlement or were insignificant villages during the Late Bronze Age. Even the cities that were destroyed around this time provide no concrete evidence that the Israelites were the conquerors. There is evidence, however, that the Sea Peoples, Egyptians (under Pharaoh Merneptah), Hittites, and some small city-states were engaging in campaigns in the region, and there is also the possibility that these strata were left by natural destructive phenomena, such as fires.

Particularly perplexing for the conquest model is that the settlements that are identified as Israelite reflect Canaanite **material culture**, not Egyptian. If the Israelites had come from four hundred years of living in Egypt, one would expect their styles, architecturally and otherwise, to be similar to Egyptian styles, as that is what they would know. Yet they are not. It is quite difficult, if not impossible, to see a difference between Israelite and Canaanite material culture. One might argue that the Israelites used local tradespeople and that explains the similarities, but this does not solve the issues related to the conquest model, which envisions the Israelites purging the land of local people and their remains. It would also be surprising for a people who had supposedly been builders in Egypt (as slave labor) to require external (non-Israelite) workers.

Furthermore, as noted in the biblical objections, there is no mention of battles in the coastal plains, the most desirable territory in the region due to the fertility of the soil and the proximity to the sea. This neglect of the fertile land is also reflected in the archaeological record of the Israelites' **settlement pattern**. The earliest evidence of Israelites in the land is in central highlands, which is the least habitable area in the region due to the unforgiving terrain. This evidence negates the conquest theory, because it would be illogical to think the Israelites conquered the entire region, but chose to dwell in its least hospitable environment. Furthermore, the three hundred or so new settlements were not located on the remains of earlier dwellings, so they are not the result of conquest, but are indeed fresh locations; and the region is devoid of major Canaanite cities.

The Peaceful Infiltration Model for the Origins of Israel

In the **peaceful infiltration** model, proposed by Albrecht Alt, Martin Noth, and Yohanon Aharoni, groups of nomads, some of which originated in Egypt, moved into the central highlands and lived relatively peacefully with their neighbors until they were strong enough to do battle with them. Because these skirmishes were the most recent part of the Israelite's history, they formed the basis of their origin story. The various tribes did not all come from Egypt, some came from the surrounding new land itself (perhaps due to a religious conversion to **Yahwism**). Rather than a large, fully formed people group who all resettled at the same time, this theory proposes that the nation of Israel developed as a loose federation of tribes over a long period of history for mutually beneficial reasons. (Some tribes may have even been enemies or rivals at earlier points in time.)

Biblical Arguments in Favor of the Peaceful Infiltration Model

The peaceful infiltration model resembles the portrayal of early Israel in the book of Judges. In Judges the Israelites live in the land surrounded by other people groups; sometimes conflicts arise and the Israelites are conquered or defeated, and at other times they are victorious. Joshua 23:4 also refers to them living in the land among the nations that remain. This is similar to the early origin legends in Genesis, which have the first Hebrew families coming from outside the land to live alongside those of the land. Joshua 9 and 24 both describe incidents in which the Israelites make a treaty with others, demonstrating a willingness to live peacefully with those who already inhabit the land.

Archaeological Arguments in Favor of the Peaceful Infiltration Model

This theory fits the settlement pattern (discussed in the archaeological arguments above) of the Israelites beginning in the central highlands and slowly moving toward the better territories. It accounts for the small rural villages in the least desirable part of the region rather than evidence of resettling major destroyed cities. The new housing style and slight pottery variation could indicate the outside influence of a people group not native to the region. This model also explains why some cities are destroyed, while others are not.

Biblical Arguments against the Peaceful Infiltration Model

The obvious argument against this theory is the total destruction described in the first half of the book of Joshua. Some proponents of the peaceful infiltration model will argue that since the battles are the most recent part of Israel's history, they are the best remembered, and the first half of Joshua reflects this more recent phase of their history. Depending on one's view of the redaction history of the final form of the Bible, this defense has some challenges, including the ones mentioned with the previous model.

Archaeological Arguments against the Peaceful Infiltration Model

This theory relies on large groups of people living in the desert for extended periods of time prior to settling the land (as the population in the central highlands increased from 12,000 to 55,000). Not only is there no explanation for where these people would come from, but this would not have been possible without camels, which weren't domesticated until the tenth century BCE at the earliest. In addition, the version of **nomadism** that this theory envisions—people moving from place to place with no fixed settlements—is not known in this part of the world at this time. The biblical text does describe transhumance pastoralism—seasonal nomadism mixed with fixed settlements—but this lifestyle involves a fixed settlement.

The Peasant Revolt or Resettlement Model for the Origins of Israel

In the **peasant revolt** or resettlement theories, a group of escaped slaves come from Egypt and connects with oppressed peasants who already live in the land. Upon hearing the narrative of the escaped slaves, the peasants join the slaves and adopt their story. They settle into the central highlands and gradually take over the land. In the peasant revolt versions proposed by George Mendenhall and Norman Gottwald,[4] the peasants join the slaves because they too are oppressed by the city-state system and want to cast off the yoke of their oppressors. While called a revolt, this was not necessarily a violent uprising, but rather an abandonment of their local king and a resettling in the highlands, which is a good location to avoid chariots and other military machinery. At times, whole cities may have converted and joined the movement.

The **resettlement model** has the same basic premise as the peasant revolt, but the reason for the migration is the unexpected societal collapse that occurred in the ancient Near East around 1200 BCE. At the end of the Late Bronze Age, nine civilizations (Minoans, Myceneans, Hittites, Babylonians, Egyptians, Canaanites, Cypriots,

---

4. These two scholars did not agree and proposed very different sociological models for understanding why the peasants joined the slaves, but at their cores their models follow the same structure and have similar arguments for and against, so they are treated here as one model.

Mahtani, and Assyrians) either collapsed or declined severely. This led to the first dark age in history, and the world would not see another collapse of this scale until the fall of the Roman Empire. There is no known cause. The classic explanation is that a drought led to famine, which led to the migration of the Sea People (six people groups of unknown origin), which wreaked havoc on the trade routes, finally leading to societal collapse, but today scholars find this explanation overly simplistic (but not necessarily inaccurate).[5] This societal power vacuum, so the theory goes, created a target-rich environment for a small and relatively powerless group to gain a foothold in the land and eventually develop into a nation.

Biblical Arguments in Favor of the Peasant Revolt or Resettlement Model

When reading the Bible against the grain, Exodus 12:38 helps support this theory. After a series of plagues, many of which distinguish between Israelites and others and set them apart, Exodus 12:38 states that Israelites (here called the Hebrews) left Egypt with a mixed crowd. This description does not fit with the author's primary concern, which is to set the Hebrews apart as God's chosen people; therefore, it is more likely to contain a historical element—that the Israelites were comprised not only of Hebrews. Numbers 11:4 also refers to a group of non-Israelites among them. Some have suggested that the Founding Family narratives (Genesis 12–50) were constructed to unify diverse groups, for example, in a geographical clustering, which could indicate different tribal connections to the lands. Finally, the migration of the tribe of Dan from the plains to the hill country of Galilee as described in Judges 17–18 seems to fit this pattern better than the other two options.

One other biblical passage has been used to support this theory of peasant revolt or resettlement. The verse comes from Judges 5, usually considered one of the oldest passages in the Hebrew Bible (the older a textual element is the more likely it is to reflect the historical realities of the time it describes). Judges 5:8 talks about the people choosing "new gods" and going to war. This is a confusing statement in a victory

---

5. For an excellent, detailed discussion of the collapse and the reasons for it, see, Eric Cline, *1177 BC: The Year Civilization Collapsed* (Princeton: Princeton University Press, 2014).

song for Yahweh. It could be that this is a reference to the tribes who chose to convert and become Yahwists and part of Israel. Ezekiel 16:3 claims that the nation's origins were in the land of Canaan, and Isaiah 19:18 says five Canaanite cities converted to Yahwism.

Archaeological Arguments in Favor of the Peasant Revolt or Resettlement Model

The arguments in favor of the peaceful infiltration model also apply to these models. In addition to these previous arguments, one can add two items from Egyptian archaeology. The first is a series of reliefs from the Karnak temple. These reliefs detail an Egyptian campaign against three cities and one people group; one of the cities is labeled Ashkelon. Egyptian drawing is quite specific and distinguishes humans according to their nationalities (Hittites, Sea Peoples, and even distinguishing between the various types of Sea Peoples, Canaanites, etc.); the Egyptians are careful to preserve differences. In the **Karnak reliefs**, there is no physical distinction between the people group and the Canaanites of the cities; this indicates the Egyptians believed this group and the Canaanites to be the same people. It is likely these reliefs should be paired with a second Egyptian artifact, the **Merneptah Stele**. The reasons for interpreting these two Egyptian remains together is that they both depict the same Pharaoh (Merneptah) conquering three cities (the first of which is named Ashkelon on both artifacts) and a group of people. It is reasonable, therefore to assume these are two different depictions of the same military campaign. The stele

The Merneptah Stele, which currently resides in the Cairo Museum, recounts a military campaign by Pharaoh Merneptah against the *cities* of Ashkelon, Gezer, and Yanoam, and the *people* of Israel (enlarged).

claims victories against Ashkelon, Gezer, Yanoam, and the people of Israel (which would mean Israel is also the people group in the Karnak reliefs); it is clear that the hieroglyphics here indicate a "people group" and not "city." These artifacts offer extrabiblical evidence that a people group known to the Egyptians as "Israel" existed in the central highlands, but they were not yet considered a nation or even a city-state, and the Egyptians made no distinction between Israelites and Canaanites. This lends credibility to the idea that most of the Israelites are actually converted Canaanites rather than a totally separate group that originated out of Egypt.

Finally, the resettlement model fits with the known sociological phenomenon in the Late Bronze Age. The Hittite and Assyrian empires were declining and weak. Egypt had defended itself first against the Hittites and then the emerging Sea Peoples; they were successful but battered. After being rebuffed in Egypt, the Sea Peoples were settled in the coastal plains region. In addition, there was chaos and bickering among the small city-states within the Southern Levant, as known from the Amarna letters.[6] This social disruption created the perfect environment for a newly formed group to settle on undesirable land and gain a base from which to expand.

Biblical Arguments against the Peasant Revolt or Resettlement Model

No major biblical tradition can be used to support either of these theories. This is particularly true of the Exodus, which in the Bible is portrayed as the origin of the nation of Israel and its relationship to its God. In both theories, the Exodus plays a minor, almost secondary role. Though much of the narrative detail of the Exodus is likely theological rather than historical, the idea that the core of these

---

6. Discovered in Amarna, Egypt (formerly Akhetaten, the capital city of the eighteenth-dynasty Pharaoh Akhenaten), the Amarna letters are a collection of diplomatic and administrative texts detailing correspondence between Egypt and Egyptian representatives in Canaan during the New Kingdom. The 'apirū/Habiru is a socially marginalized group described in the Amarna Letters (debtors, slaves, etc.—EA 288), but they were not a homogeneous ethnic group. The letters claim that some had become mercenaries and plunderers who roved in bands. They were independent and usually sided with whomever was most advantageous for them. At times, they are linked to the 'ibrî, which was a group known as "those who've crossed over." These minor rebellions from members of a socially oppressed group demonstrate the sentiment of the region.

original settlers were once slaves in Egypt seems essential to the narrative's historical origins, as no one in history has ever fabricated an origin story in which God's chosen began as slaves; usually, myths of origin claim the people are children of a god or gods.

Archaeological Arguments against the Peasant Revolt or Resettlement Model

These theories highlight the motivation for the migration—they address "who" more than "how" and "why" more than "what." Both theories make few specific, historical claims regarding dates, places, and peoples. Thus it is harder to argue against them from an archaeological frame. The one objection to the peasant revolt model is that it is based on modern sociological theory that is not reflected elsewhere in the ancient Near East.[7] Gottwald, in particular, saw the people who eventually comprise Israel ideologically, in that he framed his theory in terms of workers throwing off the yoke of their oppressors. While there was a widespread societal collapse at this time, there is no evidence this was caused by those in the lower classes attempting to eliminate or escape the hierarchal structure of the city-state system. Furthermore, many of the early settlements were close to Canaanite cities, which does not support the idea of intentional separation.

Mendhall, on the other hand, took a less ideological and more theological approach, as he viewed Yahwism as the catalyst for the new nation. Here, too, an objection could be made, because these early settlements contain no cultic buildings, no temples, sanctuaries, high places, altars—indeed, no religious architecture at all. Both theories propose that the people of the land abandoned their traditional beliefs and joined the worship of Yahweh the Liberator. Given the important role of Israelite religion in both the biblical texts and these theories, the absence of religious artifacts in these early settlements is highly perplexing.

Final Thoughts

From this extended example, one can see how both biblical studies and archaeology factor into a biblical archaeology answer to a

---

7. The later Jewish Revolts (66–73 CE) might fit this sociological model, but this is a much later cultural phenomenon than Israel's origins.

historical question. Both fields contribute evidence to the proposed solutions and both fields are used in critiquing each theory. This intricate dance between the two disciplines connects the past with the modern interpreter's ability to access that past.

Why does the answer matter? In this case it goes to the heart of who the Israelites were, which is of vital importance to both archaeologist and biblical scholar. If either of the first two theories are correct, then the Israelites are a foreign people who come into the land with their religion in place. But, if either version of the final theory is accurate, then the Israelites are mostly Canaanites who came from the land and must have gone through a process of cultural and religious dissonance from those who did not join their revolt. Imagine reading a biblical text containing a prohibition of Asherah worship and picture how different one's interpretation would be if the exegete believes the Israelites being admonished were Yahwists from the start, with a long history with this God in contrast to a group of relatively recent converts. The answer to this question has an effect on one's interpretation of every single related biblical passage. For this reason, it is one of the most important questions in both fields and requires still more discernment before it can be sufficiently answered.

It is tempting to want archaeology to "prove" or "disprove" the Bible, but what archaeology actually does is help one understand how the Bible came to say what it says; and that, in turn, helps one understand and appreciate the biblical message more fully. Regarding the origins of Israel, thoughtful believers over the centuries have wrestled with the question of how a loving God could have led the Israelites to exterminate the local Canaanite population and seize their land. Archaeology shows that the biblical depiction of a foreign population killing and driving out the local population is inaccurate: if something like that occurred at all, it was a small part of a much more complex chain of events. Armed with this information, the biblical interpreter is in a position to ask more meaningful questions of the text, such as, why did the writers of these texts feel the story of their people's origin must have or should have been like this? What does this say about the religious beliefs of the writers? What theological perspective led them to "remember" their origins in this way? In effect, even when archaeology does not "explain" the Bible, knowledge of archaeology enables the biblical interpreter to ask more appropriate and more meaningful questions of the text.

Questions for Review and Discussion

1. What are some other important questions for biblical archaeology—questions with a historical component that could be asked of both archaeologists and biblical scholars?

2. Which model for the origins of ancient Israel do you find most convincing and why?

3. Do you think you might be biased in favor of certain kinds of evidence or against certain other kinds of evidence? Explain why you believe this is, or is not, the case.

4. What makes the question about Israel's historical origins so important for an archaeologist? What makes it important for a biblical scholar?

Key Terms

conquest model
context
dialogue
household gods
Karnak reliefs
material culture
Merneptah Stele
nomadism

peaceful infiltration
peasant revolt
pillar figurines
reading against the grain
resettlement model
settlement pattern
Yahwism

Further Reading

Cline, Eric. *1177 BC: The Year Civilization Collapsed.* Princeton: Princeton University Press, 2014.

Dever, William G. *What Did the Biblical Writers Know and When Did They Know It?* Grand Rapids: Eerdmans, 2001.

Finkelstein, Israel, and Amihai Mazar. *The Quest for the Historical Israel: Debating Archaeology and the History of Early Israel.* Atlanta: Society of Biblical Literature, 2007.

GLOSSARY OF TERMS

Ages (Stone, Bronze, Iron, etc.) Distinct periods of prehistory and history.

William Foxwell Albright The late Johns Hopkins professor and former director of the William F. Albright Institute for Archaeological Research, affectionately referred to by some as the dean of biblical archaeology.

ancient parallels Texts or inscriptions from the ancient Near East that share a theme or motif with a biblical text.

archaeology Social science investigating the remains of human history (and prehistory).

areas Series of squares excavated side by side on an archaeological dig.

artifacts Physical objects uncovered during excavation.

American Schools of Oriental Research (ASOR) Professional society focused on the archaeology of the ancient Near East.

Bible Collection of texts from the ancient Near East that are revered by some as scripture.

biblical Something originating from or associated with the Bible.

Biblical Archaeology Review Archaeological magazine featuring articles written by scholars for nonspecialists. Focuses on archaeology relating to the Bible in some aspect.

biblical studies Academic discipline that investigates the Bible in its literary and historical contexts.

British Royal Engineers Division of the British Army intended to provide engineering support to British military endeavors. Several members of the British Royal Engineers made important contributions to the early history of ancient Near Eastern archaeology.

baulks Earth that remains unexcavated around the edge of an excavated square to preserve the stratigraphy of the site for future generations.

cognate Languages that share a common origin.

colophon A bookmaker's mark, usually found at the end of a text.

conquest model Theory viewing the origins of Israel according to the biblical book of Joshua (mostly, though not completely) as arising from a blitzkrieg-style war in which the Hebrews, former Egyptian slaves, killed all of the inhabitants of the land.

context Factors surrounding a word, thought, or idea that create the setting for its proper understanding.

data Facts or statistics.

database A computerized data-holding system that allows the data to be accessed in a variety of ways.

Dead Sea Scrolls Collection of ancient scrolls (c. 150 BCE–70 CE) discovered in a series of caves (preserved within large *pithos* jars) above archaeological excavations at Qumran, Israel, near the Dead Sea. These texts contain versions of the books found in the Hebrew Bible but are not limited to biblical texts.

destruction layer/stratum An archaeological level that was created by the destruction (either natural or otherwise) of the site (in whole or part) and usually preserves artifacts *in situ*.

William Dever Former director of the William F. Albright Institute for Archaeological Research and currently a professor at Lycoming College. Once one of the leading voices against the name *biblical archaeology*.

diagnostic sherds Pieces of broken pottery, rims, handles, and bases, from which the original vessel can be recreated.

dialogue Use of the latest data from multiple fields to better understand an interpretive question.

director(s) Person(s) or persons leading the excavation staff.

Ebla Archaeological site in Syria in which excavation caused controversy regarding the practice of biblical archaeology.

excavation (expedition or dig) Organized removal of earth to uncover objects from the past with the goal of learning about the civilizations that previously inhabited the site.

exegesis Reading meaning "out of" a text.

exegete One who performs exegesis.

faith Belief without proof in religious tenants.

feature A fixed archaeological find, such as a wall or built-in oven.

field school A hands-on classroom taking place on an excavation.

finds (common v. special) Removable artifacts uncovered in an excavation. Common finds are those regularly found throughout a dig (such as sherds, flint, bones, and shells); special finds are unusual or irregular discoveries (such as a whole vessel or a human skeleton).

formulaic phrase A series of exact words used to evoke a particular understanding from the reader or to provide clues to the writing's genre.

genre Style or literary category of a written piece.

hermeneutics Reading strategy used for interpretation.

historiography A genre of writing with a historical setting but the purpose of which is persuasion rather than description.

history An accurate (and ideally objective) account of the events of the past.

household gods Figurines used to represent deities, used for family worship in the home.

humanities Academic disciplines relating to the study of human culture and civilization.

imaging technology Advanced methods used to create, imitate, or reproduce an object, usually resulting in a digital image.

installations Fixed features discovered on an archaeological excavation.

interdisciplinary Use of more than one discipline in developing a theory, idea, or interpretation.

interpretation Attempt to explain the meaning of something.

intersection Point at which two disciplines overlap in their data; the arena in which interdisciplinary dialogue takes place.

Karnak reliefs Series of pictorial battle descriptions found on a wall in the Egyptian temple at Karnak.

Kathleen Kenyon British archaeologist who introduced the horizontal method (also known as the Wheeler-Kenyon method) of excavating to Syro-Palestinian archaeology during her excavations at Jericho.

literary features Devices and structures used by authors to help readers understand and interpret their work.

literary patterns (inclusio, chiasm, acrostic) Formulas used to convey meaning through the way a literary piece is structured.

locus (loci) Place or spot within a square. Can refer to features or installations or sections of earth. Each locus is given a unique number to help researchers determine the precise location of finds within an excavation.

Masoretic Text Primary version of the Tanak used for translation. Dates between the seventh and tenth centuries CE.

material culture Physical remains, such as objects, buildings, and spaces, that were used by a civilization.

Merneptah Stele Large stone plaque from the reign of Egyptian King Merneptah (1213–1203 BCE) detailing a series of battles he won and naming Israel among the peoples he conquered.

Carol Meyers Leading field-archaeologist and biblical scholar, along with her spousal colleague. She is also a Duke University professor and past president of the Society of Biblical Literature.

Eric Meyers A four-time past president of the American Schools of Oriental research and Duke University professor, known, along with his spousal colleague, as a leading field archaeologist of the current era.

myths 1. Something that might be widely believed but is not completely accurate. 2. Legends that were common in a region and the various cultural expressions of their larger metamyth.

nomadism Phenomenon in which people move from place to place without fixed settlements.

occupation layers A single stratum that was inhabited at more than one time. The original occupation layer is the oldest. The reused or repurposed inhabitation is the newer layer.

Palestinian Exploration Fund A society founded in 1865 in London with the purpose of studying the Levant.

peaceful infiltration Theory about the origins of Israel that a group of Hebrew slaves who escaped from Egypt settled in the less desirable hill region and after some treaties and minor battles eventually took over the land that became known as Israel.

peasant revolt Theory about the origins of Israel postulating that a small group of escaped slaves came from Egypt and connected with oppressed local peasants who joined the former slaves because they too were oppressed by the city-state system and wanted to cast off the yoke of their oppressors.

William Matthew Flinders Petrie Archaeological pioneer credited with the discovery of sequence dating and with refining archaeology into a discipline.

pillar figurines Small clay images depicting a female head and chest, but with a base like a tree trunk.

pottery washing and sorting Daily activity of scrubbing the sherds and identifying those with diagnostic value (e.g., rims, handles, and bases), art, or writing. These special pieces are kept, while the rest are counted, cataloged, and discarded.

preconceptions Ideas or opinions one has prior to studying a topic.

pseudonymous text Writing attributed to a false name, which hides an author's true identity.

publication Process of producing a text and making it available to read.

reading against the grain Hermeneutic in which a reader looks for elements that do not fit easily with the author's viewpoint. Used to gain insight into the world behind the text.

reading communities The questions readers ask of a text will differ based on many factors, including their gender, race, culture, age, education, religion, social status, and each factor represents a distinct reading community.

redaction An editing process that can be quite extensive, completed by a series of people, and evolved over time.

registrar Person on a dig site who records all finds, loci, and features.

Reisner-Fisher method (horizontal or architectural archaeology) Archaeological method in which the primary focus of investigation is one stratum and the architecture associated with it.

resettlement model Theory about the origins of Israel, similar to that of the peasant revolt, but the reason for the migration in this model is an unexpected societal collapse that occurred in the ancient Near East around 1200 BCE. This societal power vacuum, so the theory goes, created a target-rich environment for a small and relatively powerless group to gain a foothold in the land and eventually form a nation.

science (social v. natural) The study of the nature and behavior of natural things, usually through experimentation. Natural sciences (chemistry, biology, and physics) focus on the natural world; social sciences focus on human societies.

semantic range The various meanings that one word can have.

sequence dating Association of various pottery styles with specific time periods. Allows archaeologists to date a stratum according to the pottery remains found in it.

settlement pattern Process through which a people eventually come to occupy an area or region.

sherds Pieces of broken pottery found on an excavation.

site map Detailed drawings of the excavation that include every area, square, and locus of the exposed level of stratum.

Society of Biblical Literature (SBL) Largest professional society devoted to the academic study of biblical texts and their interpretation.

spade (trowel) Hand-held triangular tool; the most used archaeological tool.

specialist Highly skilled and knowledgeable person in a subdiscipline.

squares Smaller sections, usually five meters by five meters, within the area in which the excavation is taking place.

stratigraphy (strata, stratum) Occupation layers that have built up in a site, reflecting its history.

subdiscipline A specialty within the parameters of a larger discipline. For example, Syro-Palestinian archaeology and archaeozoology are subdisciplines of archaeology.

supervisors Those who oversee a series of squares on an excavation.

survey Archaeological method that determines the locations of archaeological sites throughout a region and researches settlement issues on a large scale.

tel, tell Mound of earth formed as the result of habitation build up.

textual context Literary setting of a word, thought, story, or idea.

theological context Religious setting of a word, thought, story, or idea.

theology The study of god(s).

tools (common, large, small, technical) Mechanisms used to conduct archaeology.

topography Physical appearance (shape) of an area of land and its features.

volunteers Dig staff who have paid for the opportunity to excavate and sometimes excavate for school credit.

Wheeler-Kenyon method (vertical archaeology) Archaeological method that excavates small areas of a site (usually in five-meter by five-meter squares) with a focus on stratigraphy and daily life.

William F. Albright Institute for Archaeological Research (AIAR) Originally named the American Schools for Oriental Research, the AIAR, founded in 1900, is the oldest American research center for ancient Near Eastern studies in the Middle East.

word study Detailed examination of a word and its semantic range through all its appearances in the Bible and related cognate texts.

world behind the text World in which the author dwelt.

world in front of the text Reader's world.

world of the text World created within the text.

Yigael Yadin Leading Israeli archaeologist of his time with a knack for using the media to promote his archaeological findings and theories. Also a former deputy prime minister of Israel and chief of staff for the Israeli defense forces.

Yahwism Worship of the god Yahweh in the ancient Near East.

INDEX

Note: The abbreviations c, cap, i, m, s, t, or n that follow page numbers indicate charts, captions, illustrations, maps, sidebars, tables, or footnotes, respectively.